Caring for strangers

18/32.

£2
ge

Caring for strangers

An introduction to practical philosophy for students of social administration

David Watson

Department of Social Administration
University of Bristol

Routledge & Kegan Paul
London, Boston and Henley

First published in 1980
by Routledge & Kegan Paul Ltd
39 Store Street,
London WC1E 7DD,
Broadway House,
Newtown Road,
Henley-on-Thames,
Oxon RG9 1EN and
9 Park Street,
Boston, Mass. 02108, USA
Printed in Great Britain by
Redwood Burn Ltd
Trowbridge and Esher

British Library Cataloguing in Publication Data

Watson, David, b. 1946
 Caring for strangers. — (The international
library of welfare and philosophy).
 1. Public welfare — Philosophy
 I. Title II. Series
 361'.001   HV31   79-41163

 ISBN 0 7100 0390 0
 ISBN 0 7100 0391 9 Pbk

The relation between moral rules and society is not a contingent one. P. H. Nowell-Smith suggests that because these rules are so useful it has become difficult for us to imagine society without them. He says that robbers must have rules if robbery is to pay, whereas what ought to be said is that robbers must have rules if there is to be robbery (Phillips and Mounce, 1969, p. 21).

On the other hand,
Nil illegitimi carborundum.

Contents

Acknowledgments

A great many people have given gifts of time and skill to assist me to write this book, and I now have an opportunity at least to thank some of them. None are now strangers. Scott Meikle, Robert Pinker, Roger Montagne, Tom Campbell, David-Hillel Ruben and Lilian Cattigan were all helpers. Once again Anne Valentine and Wilma White did my typing, even when it was re-typing.

I must also thank the following editors and publishers for their permission to re-use some material previously published: the editor of 'Social Work Today', published by the British Association of Social Workers, for material from Freedom from Welfare which appeared in vol. 6, no. 8, 1975, pp. 235–8; the editor of 'The Philosophical Journal', published by the Royal Philosophical Society of Glasgow, for material from Do Children have Rights? which appeared in vol. 13, 1976, pp. 89–99; the editor of the 'Journal of Social Policy', published by Cambridge University Press, for material from Welfare Rights and Human Rights, which appeared in vol. 6, 1977, pp. 31–46.

Introduction

In recent years there has been growing recognition of the importance of moral and political ideas in the development of social policies (see, for example, George and Wilding, 1976 and Corrigan and Leonard, 1978). The importance of such ideas lies in the fact that they are thought by promoters of social change to *justify* the social policy in question. Much else may determine policy development, but moral and political ideas are usually the *reasons* for supporting change.

George and Wilding recently argued that 'it is impossible adequately to understand the views of those who write about social welfare policy without taking account also of their social values and their social and political ideas' (1976, p.vii). The same is true of the views of those who speak about social welfare policy, and of the views of those who put policy into practice. This book illustrates this general thesis by employing, in the analysis of social policies, ideas developed and developing in moral and political philosophy. Naturally, I cannot here introduce students of social policy to *all* those ideas discussed in moral and political philosophy relevant to their concerns. I don't even want to suggest that ideas discussed in other branches of philosophy are less relevant to them. What I

want to do and what can be done here is to introduce *parts*
of a body of theory and discussion which places the study of
social policy in a new, and I believe fruitful light.

There are many ways in which we can begin a discussion
of social policy, and I choose to begin from the thought that
'modern social welfare has really to be thought of as help
given to the stranger, not to the person who by reason of
personal bond commands it without asking' (Wilensky and
Lebeaux, 1965).

In Part one I begin to set this thought in context by
developing a distinction between social policy and economic
policy, as originally drawn by Kenneth E. Boulding (1967),
and enriched by Richard Titmuss (1968, 1970). Discussion
of this distinction, as originally drawn and as developed,
draws our attention to the notions of 'unilateral transfer'
and 'gift-relationship', and in general to the moral
relationships to which social policies commit us.

In so far as social policies commit us to the desirability
of certain moral relationships, they may be assessed for
social justice. Further, though we may *begin* with the
thought that 'modern social welfare has really to be thought
of as help given to the stranger', we cannot rest there
content. Much welfare provision is not made available to
complete strangers. We discriminate between strangers,
making eligibility dependent upon desert or need. For these
reasons, Part two begins with a discussion of the ideas of
social justice and discrimination, and the relation between
them. Following on from this, some of our moral views about
which strangers *deserve* help, because of what they do or
the kind of people they are, and reflected in criteria of
eligibility for provision, will be brought forward in
discussion of what Robert Pinker calls 'the work ethic'

(1974), and of what Robin Downie and Elizabeth Telfer call 'the principle of respect for persons' (1969). All of this leads on to a discussion of the value of the idea of human rights in 'a welfare rights approach' to justification of services for strangers deserving or needy.

A second reason why we cannot rest content with the thought that social welfare policies are to be understood as 'help given to the stranger' is that we set limits on forms of delivery which imply a distinction between care and control. Help beyond these limits will not be described as 'help' but as interference. Part three is therefore a discussion of limits on forms of delivery of care, focusing on unsolicited social work intervention, behaviour modification programmes and the idea of childhood, introducing philosophical discussion of the ideas of individual liberty and paternalism.

Thus I hope to introduce students of social administration, and those engaged in social studies generally, to some of the ideas of practical philosophy useful in the appraisal of social policies.

A word about how the book might be used may be helpful. My theme is the justification of policies caring for strangers, and this theme provides an opportunity for discussion of many moral issues. Each Part develops a distinct aspect of the theme, and indeed the chapters of Parts two and three are themselves relatively independent discussions. There is, then, scope for students' interests to dictate the sequence of reading. The book concludes with a Guide to further reading which gives access to other discussions of these and related ideas: you have discovered the tip of an iceberg.

Part One

Social policy and moral identity

1   Introduction

Taking counsel from Richard Titmuss (1968, p.21) we may
study social administration making welfare objectives and
social policy 'the centre of our focus of vision'. In this
our attention may be wholly or primarily directed towards
the success or failure of particular policies in achieving
welfare objectives themselves regarded as non-problematic.
On the other hand our attention may be directed towards the
welfare objectives. When we focus upon ends rather than
means, some of the perspectives of the moral and political
philosopher will be of service.

When we direct our attention towards means rather than
ends, we are usually concerned with the *efficiency* of a
particular administrative method in achieving an objective,
and not with its *moral justification.* Though, of course, some
efficient means may be argued to be not morally justified,
for example, in certain contexts, means-tested benefits.
When we direct our attention towards social policy objectives,
on the other hand, we are ususlly concerned precisely with
their moral justification. How would, or might, supporters
of a social policy aimed at a particular objective justify
its pursuit? What alternative objectives can be plausibly
morally justified? Change, as a consequence of social policy,

7

is not simply a function of the moral views of policy-makers. But it is in part. And we recognise this whenever we ask for a moral reason why we should support a policy aimed at a particular objective. The answer we get will be an attempted moral justification. Amongst other things, moral and political philosophy is the study of the plausibility of moral justifications which may be offered in defence of objectives.

Before we can turn our attention to the various moral justifications which might be offered in support of various social policy objectives, we must be a little clearer about how to recognise a social policy which might have a welfare objective. I shall next develop a distinction between social and economic policy which leads in the right direction. Very broadly, I shall argue that social, as opposed to economic policies aim to create moral relationships between individuals, giving individuals moral identities in relation to others. As the discussion develops, the distinction between social and economic policy will enable us to look specifically at our economic activities and the idea of 'alienation'. The account of social policy developed rests upon analysis of the ideas of 'unilateral transfer' and the 'gift-relationship'.

2

Social policy
and economic policy

The broad distinction I shall draw is owed to the Kenneth E.
Boulding (1967). In any attempt to distinguish social
policy, particularly by distinguishing social policy from
economic policy, it is as well to begin by noting the
following two points. First, we may distinguish a wider and
a narrower use of the expression 'social policy'. In the
wider use, to mean, say 'policy directed towards making some
change in the conditions of life in society', 'social
policies' may include economic policies. In attempting to
distinguish social policies from economic policies, we shall
be working with a narrower use of the expression. Second,
we must not expect the criteria of identity for social
policies and economic policies to classify actual policies
exclusively. The distinction is a *broad* one. Actual
policies will have social and economic elements. Boulding
illustrates a spectrum of policies ranging from at one end
policies that seem clearly economic, such as price policy,
most aspects of tax policy, and fiscal policy, to 'a whole
range of policies toward the so-called underprivileged;
relief, social security, various forms of aid to those in
need, Medicare, and so on' (1967, p.4) at the other end of
the spectrum, which seem clearly social. And yet, even at

the extremes of the spectrum, policies have both economic
and social elements. Price policies and fiscal policies may
be predominantly economic, but their effective implementation
depends upon social virtues such as truth-telling and promise-
keeping, and recognition of the corresponding social
obligations. Social security and Medicare may be
predominantly social policies, but they remain allocative
systems and ration demand and supply (Titmuss, 1968, p.29).

However, despite the complexities created by such
overlapping in practice, we may still venture a distinction
in theory. Here is Boulding's distinction: 'we can identify
the "grant" or unilateral transfer - whether money, time,
satisfaction, energy, or even life itself - as the
distinguishing mark of the social just as exchange or
bilateral transfer is a mark of the economic' (1967, p.7).

Boulding takes this further by saying that in economic
exchange, bilateral transfer, 'a quid is got for a quo'.
This is not always the case with social transactions; with
unilateral transfer 'what one party gives up is not
necessarily what the other party receives' (1967, p.7). The
justification of economic exchange is quite straightforward.
Tönnies gives us a neat account of the reasoning which lies
behind economic transactions:

> What I do for you, I do only as a means to effect your
> simultaneous, previous or later service for me. Actually
> and really I want and desire only this. To get something
> from you is my end; my service is the means thereto, which
> I naturally contribute unwillingly (in Titmuss, 1970,
> p.211).

There may be a kind of equality in economic exchange,
given that 'a system of exchange introduces the possibility
of a "measuring rod" - which may be money or any other

convenient commodity by which heterogeneous aggregates of
goods may be reduced to a common measure' (Boulding 1967,
p.5).

Noting this fact, we might be tempted to go on to draw
the distinction between economic and social transactions by
saying that economic transactions are equal exchanges
whereas social transactions are *unequal* exchanges (see
Gouldner, 1960, p.165). In an extravagant mood, we might
think of conceptualising this area as the 'social market'
in contradistinction to the 'economic market' (cf. Titmuss,
1968, p.22). And what we have learned is that in the social
market you may get a pretty raw deal, or you may do rather
well.

I don't think we should be so extravagant as to talk of
the 'social market'(1) nor be tempted to describe social
transactions as 'unequal exchanges'. The reasons are simple
but fundamental. First, since social transactions occur
in a segment of the social system *without* a 'measuring rod',
what is transferred cannot be of equal or unequal value. Of
course I'm not suggesting that the concept of equality has
no place in critical discussions of social policy. I shall
indeed introduce quite contrary ideas in Part two of this
book. In particular the concept comes into claims for equal
treatment for individuals of equal moral status. The point
here is just that in social transactions what is transferred
has no equal or unequal exchange value. Second, although
social transactions may or may not involve the transfer of
commodities of equal or unequal (economic) exchange value,
even when commodities are transferred the object of the
exercise is not that the parties should acquire the
commodities in question, as would be the case in economic
exchange, but rather the fulfilment of an obligation. Talk

of 'unequal exchange' in the context of social transactions obscures the distinction we are trying to clarify by assimilating social to economic transactions.

For these reasons the contrast I want to draw is best put as between transactions in which there may be equal exchange (the economic), and transactions in which, as Boulding puts it, what one party gives up is not necessarily what the other party receives (the social). And for the same reasons it would be better to talk of engaging in social *relationships* rather than social transactions, transfers or exchanges.

3   Social policy and moral obligations

Let me now develop the point that in engaging in social
relationships 'the object of the exercise is the fulfilment
of an obligation'. Again, the starting point is owed to
Boulding. He says that unilateral transfers 'are justified
by some kind of appeal to a status or legitimacy, identity
or community' (1967, p.7).

As it stands, this will not do. The same form of
justification is available for economic exchange, simply
because there are economic statuses, identities and
communities. However, if we follow Richard Titmuss and
accept that we are concerned 'with different types of moral
transactions' (1968, p.20), we have available an
interpretation of Boulding's remark which does distinguish
engaging in social relationships from economic exchange.
Social relationships and economic exchange may be
distinguished exclusively by the fact that the former and not
the latter are justified by some kind of appeal to a *moral*
status or legitimacy, identity or community.

Earlier we saw Tönnies expressing the reasoning behind
economic exchange as 'what I do for you, I do only as a
means to effect your simultaneous, previous or later service
for me'. And in the light of that reasoning we might want to

say that the economic transactions of the market-place manifest *egoism*. Titmuss is led in this direction (1970, p.13). In theory this seems to me to be correct. However, in practice, because actual economic exchanges have social elements, it seems fair to say that though economic transactions often manifest egoism, they also often manifest concern for the interests of others than the individual buyer or seller. Actual individuals engaged in economic exchange are also engaged in social relationships, for example with friends and family, and may engage in economic exchange in the interests of these others. This is not egoism. It is clear, however, that in all cases of economic exchange the individuals engaged in it do not regard the interests of each other as ends to be promoted, so they may be accused of what we might call *non-tuism*. (1)

Whether we take economic exchange to be motivated by egoism or just non-tuism is not critical. On either view economic exchange cannot be said to be justified by some kind of appeal to *moral* status or legitimacy, identity or community. And this for the simple reason that egoism and non-tuism are non-moral reasons for action. I don't want to rehearse all the arguments here, but shall go on to discuss necessary conditions of a principle being a *moral* principle, and I might say here that I believe universalisability to be one such condition not satisfied by either egoism or non-tuism. I might say briefly that in the context of this claim it is important to note that there is no fact about me which might be plausibly put forward as a reason for acting *only* in my own interests as a matter of principle. This is because any such fact might also be true of someone other than me, and a reason for me to act also in his interest. I leave you to consider your own examples (but see Williams, 1973).

Social relationships, on the other hand, *are* justified
by appeal to obligations which are moral in type. We can
begin to see this more clearly if we note that 'The
institutions with which social policy is especially
concerned, such as the school, family, church, or, at the
other end, the public assistance office, court, prison, or
criminal gang, all reflect degrees of integration and
community' (Boulding, 1967, p.7).

Within these social institutions, and in social
relationships generally, individuals are allocated statuses
or identities to which attach rights and duties in relation
to others bearing certain statuses and identities. That is,
the individuals are integrated in a system of reciprocal
obligations determined by their social identity. That is
why I said earlier that in engaging in social relationships,
the object of the exercise is the fulfilment of an
obligation. Titmuss makes no attempt to justify his calling
such reciprocal obligations 'moral'. Perhaps this is the
wisest course. Moral philosophers by no means all agree
about the definition of 'moral' (see Wallace and Walker,
1970). However, I shall call these reciprocal obligations
'moral obligations' because they are entailed by principles
which possess characteristics often regarded as at least
necessary conditions, and which also may be jointly
sufficient conditions, for being a *moral* principle. For
example, my obligations to my parents, as a son, are entailed
by the principle that children ought to show respect for their
parents. Again, a judge's obligations to a defendant include
those entailed by the principle that all accused men ought to
receive a fair trial. The conditions satisfied by these
principles are that, first, they are universalisable. That

is, if I maintain that I ought to do X, then I am committed
to maintaining that anyone else ought to do X unless there
are relevant differences between the other person and myself,
or between his situation and mine (see Wallace and Walker,
1970, p.8). Neither egoism nor non-truism satisfy this
necessary condition and so are not *moral* points of view.
This is because there must be occasions when there may be no
relevant difference between you and me. But in that case,
if you ought to do X in whatever circumstances prevail,
then, given universalisability, so ought I. But X may be
an action in your interests and either not in my interests
or indeed harmful to my interests. And this is incompatible
with egoism, which declares that one ought only to do what
is in one's own interests. And it is also incompatible with
non-tuism, which declares that one ought only to do what
is in the interests of others than you. Second, the
principles are action-guiding. Third, the principles may
broadly, though obscurely, be described as aiming at human
well-being. Entailed by moral principles, the social
obligations in question are thus moral obligations, and the
corresponding statuses, identities and communities 'moral'.

Note that I claim only that these social relationships
are moral as opposed to non-moral. Some of them, therefore,
may be *im*moral. Some relationships which are moral in kind
are morally objectionable. From some moral points of view,
for example, widespread traditional moral relationships
between husbands and wives, or between parents and children,
are immoral. The relationships are governed by principles
which are universalisable, action-guiding, and aim at human
well-being, but, from the critical moral point of view,
perhaps the conception of human well-being is flawed. To
put it mildly, in these cases what one party gives up is not

necessarily what the other party receives.

Social relationships, then, may be distinguished exclusively from economic exchange, transfer or transaction, in being justified by some kind of appeal to a moral status or identity.

4
Moral obligations to strangers

In the Introduction to this book I said I would begin by
setting in context the thought that 'modern social welfare
has really to be thought of as help given to the stranger,
not to the person who by reason of personal bond commands
it without asking'. This I have begun to do, using the work
of Boulding and Titmuss, and will now take further. In his
own attempts to draw the boundaries of social policy Titmuss
suggests a distinction, among social relationships, between
'face-to-face' and 'stranger' relationships. 'Face-to-face'
relationships are 'the reciprocal rights and obligations of
family and kinship' (1970, p.212). 'Stranger' relationships
on the other hand, arise from 'processes, institutions and
structures which encourage or discourage the intensity and
extensiveness of anonymous helpfulness in society' (1970,
p.212).

For Titmuss 'stranger' relationships are the chief
concern (but thus not the sole concern) of social policy.
Like Boulding, Titmuss sees social relationships as an
'integrative system'; 'stranger' relationships presumably
integrating members of a society who are otherwise unknown
to each other, through anonymous (at least intended)
helpfulness.

Titmuss describes both sorts of social relationship as a *gift-relationship*. This can be misleading since 'within all such gift transactions of a personal face-to-face nature lie embedded some elements of moral enforcement or bond' (1970, p.210).

These 'gifts' are obligatory. However, the word may pick out the fact that moral obligations are freely entered into. Titmuss (1970, p.212) follows Mauss (1970) in claiming that social gifts to 'anonymous others' 'carry no explicit right, expectation or moral enforcement of a return gift'. There is no moral obligation to give in return nor, I think he would add, was the first gift obligatory.

It might seem from this that Titmuss would deny my earlier claim that social relationships may be distinguished as justified by appeal to moral *obligations* - for social gifts to strangers are not theirs by right. But this is not so. Following G.R. Grice (1967), he draws a distinction between contractual and 'ultra' moral obligations. Rights correspond to the former but not the latter. Titmuss regards all social gifts to 'strangers' as a matter of moral obligation, but only as 'ultra-obligatory'. That is, as a matter of self-fulfilment through devotion to others (see Grice, 1967, p.169ff).

It seems to me that Titmuss makes a serious mistake in asserting that *all* social gifts to 'strangers' fulfil only 'ultra-obligations'. The 'strangers' in question are not wholly 'anonymous others'. We know they are fellow-*men*. It seems to me that if we know the 'strangers' to be human, we have certain moral duties towards them and they have corresponding rights. There are certain needs which are 'basic' in the sense that their satisfaction is something any man has reason to want if he wants anything, given the

conditions of human life (see Foot, 1967, ch. 6). Rights
to the satisfaction of these basic needs are traditionally
called 'natural' or 'human' rights. Satisfaction of such
needs is not a matter of 'ultra-obligation' but of our basic
contractual moral obligations to 'the society of humanity
as a whole' (as Grice notes, 1967, p.150ff). Thus the claim
that social relationships may be distinguished as justified
by appeal to moral obligations stands, but now we recognise
that *non-basic* gifts to 'strangers' may be only 'ultra-
obligatory'. Basic gifts are theirs by right.

My objection to Titmuss's account of social gifts to
'strangers' has an advantage in practice. 'Ultra-obligatory'
gifts, being a matter of individual self-fulfilment, are
difficult to predict and co-ordinate. Since basic human
needs can be identified, those gifts to 'strangers' which
aim to satisfy them are more easily regulated by social
policy (see Watson, 1977).

Having noted but restricted Titmuss's modification of
the claim that social relationships may be distinguished
exclusively from economic exchange in being justified by
some kind of appeal to a moral status or identity, we might
usefully remove one other objection which lurks in the
background of the works of the writers we have been
considering.

It might be pointed out that social reciprocities
'actually mobilize egoistic motivations and channel them
into the maintenance of the social system...there is an
altruism in egoism, made possible through reciprocity'
(Gouldner, 1960, p.173). Or again, it might be said that
'uncertainty about the nature of obligations arising out of
social exchange also brings a measure of stability to social
relationships....Social exchange can also function to

establish domination or superiority over others' (Pruger,
1973, p.291). Or, lastly, it might be claimed of social
'transactions' that 'the object of the exchange was to
produce a friendly feeling between the two persons concerned,
and unless it did this it failed of its purpose' (Mauss,
1970, p.18).

But if social relationships are intended to serve self-
interest, they are manifestations of egoism and it is *false*
that social relationships may be distinguished exclusively
from economic exchange by the form of their justification.

However, this would be the wrong conclusion to draw from
the sociologist's and anthropologist's observations. Social
relationships may *function* in the ways described, but it
doesn't follow at all that what is thus brought about was
a *purpose* of, or *intended* by the participants. And therefore
it does not follow for social relationships that
'manifestations of altruism in this sense' should 'be thought
of as self-love' (Titmuss, 1970, p.212). Our distinction
stands.

5   Economic
policy and alienation

Corresponding to the broad distinction drawn between
economic exchange, etc. and engaging in social relationships,
we may draw the promised distinction between social policy
and economic policy: *social policy, unlike economic policy,
is justified by some kind of appeal to a moral status or
identity.* I now turn to a discussion of consequences of our
economic activities other than the transfer of commodities
of exchange value. As I said earlier, the consequences I
have in mind may be thought of as forms of 'alienation'.

Given what has been said about the form of justification
appropriate to social policy, we should expect that 'By and
large it is an objective of social policy to build the
identity of a person around some community with which he is
associated' (Boulding, 1967, p.7).

That is, an objective is to build a moral identity, the
details of that identity varying with the social policy in
question, but always a moral identity through which
individuals are engaged in social relationships as *human
beings* having a certain status in relation to each other.
We may have social relationships with animals other than
man, but the social relationships with which we are here
concerned are relationships consciously engaging our

fellow-*men*. If, as I suggested earlier, there are certain
needs which are 'basic', in the sense that their satisfaction
is something any human being has reason to want if he wants
anything, then the statuses and identities offered in social
relationships are offered to individuals with these basic
needs, and with the corresponding human rights possessed by
all members of 'the society of humanity as a whole'. Of
course, in addition we may engage in social relationships
with particular individuals because of their possession of
valued characteristics other than those served by the
satisfaction of basic needs (see Watson, 1970). Social
policy, self-consciously engaging men in social relationships,
draws our attention towards these facts, facts of their
humanity, which are sufficient to assign to the individuals
concerned a moral status and identity as human beings.

Contrast the identities and statuses offered by economic
exchange:

Under ordinary circumstances the exchange is impersonal...
requiring no special effort or attention from either buyer
or seller. Once the exchange has taken place, there is
no residue or accumulation of unfulfilled obligations, and
thus no inherent dynamic to extend the relationship beyond
the time contractually specified (Pruger, 1973, p.290).

The economic relationship is temporally restricted to the
period until the exchange is complete, and, most importantly,
offers the individuals concerned severely restricted
identities. The relationship is *impersonal*. The individuals
are identified *only* as buyer and seller. As Tönnies noted,
each may say 'to get something from you is my end'. Neither
has any further interest in the other. In so far as economic
exchange offers a relationship between individuals regarded
only as a source of commodities, it is not a relationship

between human beings: the individual participants are not
recognised as having that status or identity.

This gives us further insight into the reasons why
economic policy, motivated by egoism or perhaps non-tuism,
is non-moral. It asks us to not conceive of the relationships
it governs as relationships between human beings. It asks
us not to regard the individuals participating in economic
exchange, to use Kantian language, as ends-in-themselves. It
disregards even their basic social relationship founded on
their common humanity. The participants are, literally,
alien.

It might be said, by way of objection to this way of
developing the distinction between economic and social policy,
that social as well as economic relationships may assign
to individuals restricted identities. For example,
individuals engaged in social relationships as 'child',
'wife', 'priest' and so on, have social identities which
may severely restrict their rights and duties (see Holt,
1974). We must not exaggerate this. Some of the restrictions
are open to negotiation because they are identities adopted
in a wide range of ways. The important point here is that
however closely related to a set of rights and duties, social
identities are identities relating fellow-*men*, that is,
relating individuals whose identity is not so far restricted
as to deny them moral status as human beings, nor therefore,
so resticted as to deny them the capacity to enter into
other kinds of social relationship. In presupposing the basic
moral status of participants, social relationships are
relatively open-ended.

The present extension of the distinction between economic
and social policy is useful in providing a framework for the
description of certain consequences of our economic activities

as forms of 'alienation'. In an orthodox socialist critique
of our capitalist economic activities, (1) modern forms of
alienation have as their root cause the institution of wage-
labour, in which one man is forced to sell his labour power
to another, his employer. The labourer no longer has access
to the means of production and the means of subsistence.
What he shall produce and subsist on is in the control of
another. The labourer is not free to do what he wants at
work. The employer is master of his activity: his capacity
to perform creative work is thwarted and distorted to suit
his employer's ends. Nor is fulfilment possible during
leisure time, thanks to the commercialisation of leisure,
and the provocation of artificial dissatisfactions divorced
from genuine human needs, all to promote sales. Perhaps
the worst form of alienation of all comes from the extreme
division of labour. We lose the capacity to communicate
with fellow-men who occupy a different economic role.

Whatever we think of the relationship between this
critique and our own economic activities, it falls within
the theoretical framework provided by the account developed
of the nature and implications of economic exchange. The
institution of wage-labour disregards their basic social
relationship as fellow-men, and assigns to the individuals
concerned an economic relationship and identities only as
'labourer' and 'employer'. The employer is encouraged to
treat the labourer merely as a means to his own ends, and
not as an end-in-himself. The commercialisation of leisure,
and so on, are not designed to offer scope for self-
fulfilment, but only to offer the 'producer' an alternative
identity as 'consumer'. A socialist critique of capitalist
economic activity can, then, be understood as drawing
criticism towards the severely restricted identities such

forms of economic activity offer to participants. The
identities offered are 'restricted' because the individuals
are denied access to, and control of, the means of production
and subsistence.

What a socialist critique often fails to bring out in its
criticism of capitalism, though the points about communication
may lead in this direction, is that capitalist economic
activity, *like all forms of economic activity*, offers only
economic relationships. As we have seen, participants in
such relationships are alien to each other. In economic
relationships individuals bear identities which disregard
their moral status and identity as human beings. The
socialist critique of capitalism laments the individual's
loss of economic autonomy, but we might also lament the
alienation in the loss of *social* identities. Access to and
control of the means of production and subsistence will not
be an end of alienation, precisely because men remain
engaged only in economic relationships.

Our extension of the distinction between economic and
social policy thus gives insight into a typical socialist
critique of capitalist economic activity, but also shows
limitations it may incorporate. This can be further
illustrated if we look at the account of 'exploitation'
implied in the critique: transactions involving an exchange
of things of unequal value (Gouldner, 1960, p.166). Since
social goods have no exchange value, this can only be an
account of *economic* exploitation. Perhaps economic autonomy
will end economic exploitation, but to understand the
possibility of either we need to recognise the existence
of social relationships between individuals' assigned
identities which oblige some to give and entitle others to
receive unequally in economic exchange. To understand

economic exploitation we must note the general consequences
of economic exchange for social relationships. Economic
exchange is impersonal. It disregards our social and moral
status, encouraging individuals to accept non-human
identities, and thus even come to accept forms of economic
exchange which deny them their basic *human* needs. More
often, they are encouraged to accept restricted social
identities which support unequal economic exchange. Economic
exploitation is sustained by forms of alienation which are
social, and which may be partly determined by, but are also
a determinant of, access to means of production and
subsistence.

6

Social
policy and integration

The description of certain consequences of our economic
activities as forms of alienation followed from the
distinction drawn earlier between social policy and economic
policy. Given that economic exchange embodies forms of
alienation, an objective for social policy comes clearly
into view. And once again we can describe it by quoting
from Boulding: 'social policy has to concern itself
profoundly with questions of identity and alienation' (1967,
p.7).

Social policy, justified by some kind of appeal to a moral
status or identity, must have as one central objective the
creation of forms of social integration as opposed to forms
of alienation. This is simply because the moral statuses
and identities in question *are* forms of social integration,
and justify such policies by being their objectives. However,
forms of social integration are many and varied. Which
forms should our social policies aim to produce?

This is a matter of moral judgment. Which is not to say
that one view may be as cogently argued as any other. We may
approach the practical question by, first, asking how social
policy is to be related to the forms of alienation embodied
in our economic activities. Solutions to practical questions

cannot be given wholly in general terms, but strategies
described in such terms will show their place in the
theoretical framework so far developed. Our social policies
may aim to match specific forms of alienation with support
for specific forms of social integration. Services
compensating diswelfares generally may be regarded as social
policies ameliorating the effects of economic policies,
demanding that the individuals responsible recognise the
sufferers as fellow-men whose social interests have been
harmed.

On the other hand, we might oppose forms of alienation
more directly, attempting their elimination rather than
amelioration. Alienation caused by the extreme division of
labour might be attacked, say, by a rejection of mass
production methods which demand it or, more modestly, by
making some of the labour-force directors, and so on.

Perhaps we should avoid much professionalisation of the
social services. For although, say, the social worker-client
relationship is social, it may easily become a threat to
those capacities for self-determination necessary in
maintaining our ordinary forms of social integration.

We might approach our question about the forms of social
integration our social policies should aim to produce by,
second, noting that, as a matter of consistency, our social
policies must serve at least *basic* human needs. As I argued
earlier, we have basic moral duties to our fellow-men simply
because of their basic needs as fellow-men. Social policy,
justified by appeal to the moral statuses and identities of
its subjects, must at least aim to fulfil our basic
contractual moral obligations. The implications of this for
social policy may be developed in detail in various ways, but
clearly we must have policies promoting health and well-being

generally, including policies relating to food, clothing, housing, medical care and education.

Beyond basic contractual moral obligations the objectives of social policy are less obvious. The forms of social integration one should aim to encourage or discourage, even the extent to which one regards the encouragement or discouragement of forms of social integration as a matter for government policy, is dependent upon one's social ideals. In general terms one can say only that social policies should provide and extend opportunities for altruism in opposition to the possessive egoism of the market-place (Titmuss, 1970, p.13).

Social policy promotes *social* services. That is, services which recognise our moral status as human beings and may offer us the opportunity to adopt further moral identities. Such identities may be status-enhancing or stigmatising. Individuals with such identities are the product of our social services. It follows from my analysis that social services which offer all individuals the opportunity to adopt identities which are status-*enhancing* produce nothing of (exchange) value, but at the same time we may add, they produce something beyond price. But that is rhetoric.

Part Two

Discriminating between strangers

In Part one I declared the emphasis upon the welfare
objectives of social policies, and said that the perspectives
of the moral and political philosopher would be of service in
discussion of their *justification*. I then went on to
distinguish social from economic policies by the *form* of
their justification: social policy, unlike economic policy,
is justified by some kind of appeal to a moral status or
identity.

It is worth noting now that this account of social policy
is to some extent stipulative. I have identified a
distinctive feature of social *as opposed to economic*
policies. This feature may still be shared by many non-
economic policies we would hesitate to call social, and may
not be a feature of some policies which are often called
social. These logical possibilities remain, but cause no
difficulty. Examples of the first kind are hard to find,
and examples of the second kind may often share the feature
of moral justification. Thus policies related to increased
investment in roads, National Parks and Higher Education,
might be justified not by reference to any moral obligation
but as a matter of simply promoting a higher 'quality of
life'. But then, such policies are also often simultaneously

justified as increasing opportunities for self-realisation,
it being our moral duty to create such opportunities, and
perhaps even to take them, whenever practicable. In any
case, and this is the piece of stipulation, I shall use
'social policy' to describe policies justified in the way
identified in Part one as unavailable for economic policies.

In Part two I want to move on to discuss the kinds of
moral relationship between individuals that such social
policies might promote. I shall do this by noting various
ways in which we discriminate between strangers on moral
grounds. Our views about which moral relationships ought to
be promoted may be called our conception of *social justice*.
So I take the opportunity to begin Part two with a discussion
of the relationship between various forms of discrimination
and social justice. In the course of this discussion various
grounds for just discrimination will be mentioned, but I want
to pay special attention to *merit* or *desert* as a criterion,
through discussion of issues grouped around the relation
between social policies and 'the work ethic' and between
social policies and the principle of 'respect for persons'.
The conclusions of these discussions bring us back to
consider further justification of social policies as
promoting moral relationships between strangers having status
as fellow human beings. This will be done in the context of
an account of the relation between welfare rights and human
rights.

8   Positive discrimination and social justice

We may aim to give help to strangers by implementing social
policies, but we rarely give all strangers the same help.
Not all strangers have the same moral status, and the same
moral relationship is not offered to all. In recent years
'positive discrimination' has been the label attached to
social policies deliberately assigning higher moral status
to certain groups than to others. 'Positive discrimination'
has become a much used and effective part of social policy-
makers' public relations kit. It is 'one of those fashion-
able concepts with an aura of righteous sentiment, but little
rigorous analysis of its possible applications' (Glennerster
and Hatch, 1974, p.1). So what is *positive discrimination*?

Glennerster and Hatch give us the following part of the
history of the use of the expression:

The term owes its current popularity to the Plowden
Report, which in 1966 argued that 'the principle that
special need calls for special help should be given a new
cutting edge'. The authors of the Report had in mind
what Americans would call 'compensatory education'. It
described the process by which certain schools with
exceptionally large numbers of children who were socially
handicapped should receive extra help. It stated,
para. 151:

'We ask for "positive discrimination" in favour of such schools and the children in them, going well beyond an attempt to equalise resources. Schools in deprived areas should be given priority in many respects. The first step must be to raise the schools with low standards to the national average, the second, quite deliberately to make them better. The justification is that the homes and neighbourhoods from which many of their children come, provide little support and stimulus for learning. The schools must supply a compensating environment' (1974, p.1).

To some extent this description of positive discrimination, though taken from the Report, is misleading. It is said that positive discrimination goes 'well *beyond* an attempt to equalise resources' (emphasis mine). In the case in question the aim is to go beyond an attempt to equalise *school* resources, so that overall, when lesser home and neighbourhood support and stimulus for learning are also considered, the result will be an equalisation of resources. Better than average schools in worse than average neighbourhoods yield an equal educational opportunity.

The positive discrimination recommended by Plowden is, of course, positive discrimination on grounds of *educational need*, but the strategy can be employed in other areas of need. For example, one might support better than average investment in housing design and repair and stone-cleaning grants in city areas which are otherwise distinctly ugly – say because of factories, a gasworks or a scrapyard.

Selectivity in social services is usually recommended with the cry 'let's concentrate help on those whose needs are greatest'. Selectivity in social services is usually aimed at equalisation of individuals' resources. By concentrating

help on those whose resource needs are greatest, we can give
them a chance of satisfying their resource needs equal to that
of those whose resource needs are not so great. (1)
Positive discrimination in the case argued by Plowden, as I
have said, is also aimed at equalisation of individuals'
resources.

It is important to note, however, that there is no
conceptual link, no necessary connection between positive
discrimination, or selectivity, and the goal of equality
of individual resources. Neither positive discrimination
nor selectivity entails such an aim and might indeed be part
of policies aimed at *greater inequalities* of individual
resources.

The contingency of its relationship with the goal of
equality of individual resources goes some way towards
explaining the popularity of the notion of 'positive
discrimination' and its appeal to politicians of the Left
and the Right. However, any worthwhile analysis of the
notion must recognise its relationship to social justice or
more clearly, to *comparative justice*. This is what I want
to discuss next, in order to bring out philosophical
problems which are raised in trying to describe criteria
of identity for possible applications of positive discrimination and selectivity. The logic of comparative justice
determines the range of possible applications: what I shall
try to do is reveal relevant parts of that logic. (2)

Comparative justice necessarily involves the claims of
more than one person, and requires that some sort of balance
be struck between them. The basic *principle* of comparative
justice is that like cases are to be treated alike and
different cases to be treated differently. If Sid Bonkers
gets a large share and Doris Bonkers a small share in the

distribution of the proceeds of a 'land reclamation' scheme,
comparative justice is not satisfied until we learn of some
respect in which Sid and Doris differ, that underlies and
justifies this difference in treatment. If Sid and Doris are
exactly alike in every respect, but one is given more than
the other, the discrimination in their treatment is quite
arbitrary, and *arbitrary* discrimination is the essence of
comparative *injustice*.

Now any two people (or things) will differ in *some*
respects - it will always be possible to cite *some* difference
between them in support of differences in the way they are
treated. Suppose identical twin Scotsmen are being seen for
the job of male model - for a new design for the front of a
porridge packet. It would be unjust to select Murdo rather
than Angus because *his* name but not his brother's begins with
the letter 'M'. Yet this is a respect in which they differ.
Clearly then, comparative justice requires more than that the
difference in treatment be based on differences in
characteristics. The differences between individuals that
support differences in their treatment must be *relevant*
differences, and the similarities that support similar
treatment must be *relevant* similarities. Comparative
injustice is done when individuals who are alike in every
relevant respect, not in absolutely every respect, are treated
differently, or when individuals who are different in some
relevant respect are treated alike.

The basic principle, that like cases are to be treated
alike and different cases differently is, then, only the
starting point in the analysis of comparative justice: it
needs supplementation by criteria for determining the
relevance of differences and similarities. For this reason
the basic principle is usually said to be merely a *formal*

principle of comparative or social justice, and the criteria
of relevance with which it must be supplemented in various
contexts are called *material* principles.
In the light of this analysis of comparative justice,
'positive discrimination' and 'selectivity' are clearly part
of the *vocabulary* of comparative or social justice: these
words name, I suggest, *instruments* of comparative justice,
through such policies comparative justice is done. Further,
in practice positive discrimination and selectivity must
always be tied to some material principle of comparative
justice. Plowden, as we saw, was concerned with the
principle that special *need* calls for special help, applied
to education in schools. This is one example of a material
principle of comparative justice. And it is one which is
readily (though not necessarily) linked with the goal of
equality of individual resources. As I said, these principles
supply criteria of relevance for differences and
similarities. So in this case comparative justice will be
done if people with different *needs* are treated differently,
and people with similar *needs* are treated alike.

Another example of a material principle is the principle
that special *merit* calls for special reward. In this case
comparative justice will be done if people with different
merit (once you have decided what is meritorious) are treated
differently, and those with similar merit alike. Applications
of this principle less often yield equality of individual
resources.

I said that in practice positive discrimination, and
selectivity, must be tied to some material principle of
comparative justice; I should add that they can be tied to
any. We can positively discriminate or select on grounds
determined to be relevant by *any* material principle of

comparative justice. Hence the popularity of these notions.
Parties *divide* over material principles chosen to direct
positive discrimination or selection.

I have also said that material principles of comparative
justice determine the relevance of differences and
similarities. In this way they determine the range of
possible applications of positive discrimination. Glennerster
and Hatch, as we saw, lamented the lack of analysis of the
possible applications of positive discrimination. We are
now in a position to say that *possible applications are cases
governed by material principles of comparative justice.* Any
would-be application must be justifiable by reference to such
a material principle. Thus, in education, positive
discrimination was justified by reference to the material
principle that special (educational) need calls for special
help.

This philosophical point about positive discrimination,
that possible applications are cases governed by material
principles of comparative justice, leads us to a further
important philosophical and moral problem: how are we to
choose our material principles? They obviously play a
crucial role in positive discrimination, and one would,
therefore, prefer to be in a position to justify one's
choice of principle, and so one's social policy.

Joel Feinberg (1973, p.108) suggests what he calls the
'fair opportunity' test. Material principles are justifiable
if they identify grounds for discrimination between two
individuals such that each has a fair opportunity to acquire
or avoid them, so that each is responsible for his possession
of the relevant characteristic. On this test discrimination
on grounds of skin colour and sex are unjust, since these
are characteristics the individuals concerned have had no

fair opportunity, indeed no opportunity, to acquire or avoid.

So far all seems quite reasonable. But this is not quite so clear as we might at first believe. We tend to think that the discrimination which happily comes out 'unjust' on Feinberg's test is discrimination which already exists and which would cease to exist on employing Feinberg's test. We are forgetting that discrimination (selectivity) can indeed be *positive*. If people of a certain colour or sex or whatever have been unjustly discriminated against we may want to give them *better than* equal treatment. This is particularly relevant to social policy. As S.M. Miller (in Glennerster and Hatch, 1974, p.37) puts it,

Positive discrimination can be viewed as a penalty or reparation paid by a society to right the wrongs which have been (or are being) inflicted upon particular groups in society. These wrongs have accumulated disadvantages for these groups. Ending discrimination is insufficient to change their situation; society has an obligation to repair the damages by giving preference to the discriminated. They are owed something by society. The past (and present) must be made up.

The problem this raises is as follows: positive discrimination here seems to require better than equal treatment for people of a certain colour, sex or whatever, it seems to require special treatment on grounds which the individuals have had no fair opportunity to acquire or avoid. Following Feinberg's test we declare discrimination against such individuals on those grounds unjust, but then surely discrimination in their favour on those grounds is equally *unjust*.

This problem is doubly embarrassing in relation to many social services. For example, special provision for the

physically handicapped, from the blind to those suffering
multiple sclerosis, special provision for the mentally
handicapped, from the senile to mental defectives classified
as 'idiots', *all* such special provision would seem to be
unjust. Most of these handicaps are typically things which
their sufferers have had no fair opportunity to acquire or
avoid, and so not relevant to comparative justice.

Our problems are greater in relation to these handicaps
because in these cases it is very difficult to describe
special provision as 'a penalty or reparation paid by a
society to right the wrongs which have been inflicted upon
(these) particular groups'. In these cases responsibility
for the handicap cannot typically be assigned to 'society'.
So how can society have an obligation to repair or alleviate
the damage?

Let me summarise the present issue. We are looking for a
way of choosing material principles of comparative justice.
Feinberg supplies the 'fair opportunity' test, which happily
rules 'unjust' discrimination on grounds such as colour and
sex. Unfortunately it also rules 'unjust' certain positive
discrimination we might want to defend in the area of social
provision. Let me suggest how we might resolve our problem.

It seems that we may have not taken enough care in
describing the *positive* discrimination we wish to defend.
It was described as grounded in characteristics (e.g. being
female) which the individuals concerned have had no fair
opportunity to acquire or avoid. *Because* it was described
in this way it failed Feinberg's test and came out 'unjust'.
The description, however, is inaccurate.

Our desire to defend positive discrimination in relation
to coloured people and women arises in a social context in
which discrimination *against* these groups exists (or has

recently existed) and is (or was) grounded in characteristics which the individuals have had no fair opportunity to acquire or avoid: in short, a social context in which these individuals suffered unjust discrimination. If this were *not* the case I do not think we *would* wish to defend discrimination in favour of these groups.

Because of this special context we may more accurately describe policies of positive discrimination in relation to these groups as *removing and compensating for unjust discrimination* (3) rather than as grounded in characteristics the individuals have had no fair opportunity to acquire or avoid. The latter description makes such policies unjust on Feinberg's test, the former does not. It does not do so because it is not within the scope of Feinberg's test - it refers not to a characteristic of the *individuals* (e.g. being female), but to a characteristic of their past *treatment* (its being unjust). In the past such groups were disc discriminated against on grounds which they had had no fair opportunity to acquire or avoid, treatment which was unjust on Feinberg's test. Setting right an injustice is necessarily just.

This line of argument, I think, saves policies of positive discrimination in relation to coloured people and women, and any other groups who are suffering or have suffered *unjust* discrimination at the hands of society. It may not be so successful for policies aimed at removing and compensating for 'natural' handicaps, like blindness and idiocy. Because they are 'natural' and not a consequence of comparative injustice by society, though unfortunate and often tragic, such cases are not unjust or just - they are 'the luck of the draw'. Because no one has been unjust, social policies to remove and compensate 'natural' handicaps are not a matter of justice.

This does not, of course, mean that policies of positive discrimination to remove and compensate for 'natural' handicaps cannot be implemented. What it does mean is that they are to be seen not as a matter of social or comparative *justice*, but as charity.

But this might be to concede too much. First, the distinction between 'natural' and 'socially-produced' handicaps is a little artificial - even 'natural' blindness might be usually avoidable if society hadn't failed to screen all children early enough and make remedies more easily available, and so on. So society can often be found to bear some responsibility. Second, and more importantly, we might defend positive discrimination in this area as a matter of *justice* if we believe that society has a responsibility to foster *equality*. 'Natural' handicaps are thus 'natural' inequalities which society has a responsibility to set right. Positive discrimination is a matter of justice *not* because society is thus remedying its earlier injustice, but because society is thereby upholding the principle of equality.

Positive discrimination to remove and compensate for handicaps is an implementation of the material principle that *special need calls for special help*. The relation between this material principle and the principle of equality is worth noting once more, this time because it makes positive discrimination in cases of 'natural' handicaps a matter of justice.

As Gregory Vlastos has said, since needs are often *unequal*, this principle, that special need calls for special help, 'looks like a precept of *unequal* distribution' (italics mine). However, according to Vlastos, 'it is in fact *the most perfect form of equal distribution*'. He explains this

in relation to the right to security of life and person as
follows:

Believing that this is an equal right, what do we feel
this means in cases of special need?

Suppose for instance, New Yorker X gets a note from
Murder, Inc., that looks like business. To allocate
several policemen and plainclothesmen to guard him over
the next few weeks, at a cost a hundred times greater
than the per capita cost of security services to other
citizens during the same period, is surely *not* to make
an exception to the equal distribution required by the
equal right of all citizens to the security of their life
and person; it is not done on the assumption that X has
a greater right to security or a right to greater
security.... The greater allocation of community resources
in X's favour ... is made precisely *because* X's security
rights are equal to those of other people in New York.
This means that X is entitled to the same level of police-
made security as is maintained for other New Yorkers.
Hence in these special circumstances, where his security
level would drop to zero without extra support, he should
be given this to bring his security level nearer to the
normal (in Brandt, 1962, pp.40-1).

Thus special help in cases of special need can yield equality,
in this case equality of (right to) security, and thus be a
matter of social *justice*.

Let me summarise what has been said. We began with
recognition of the need for analysis of the possible
applications of positive discrimination. I have offered an
analysis of 'positive discrimination', and of 'selectivity'
which gives them a place within a theory about comparative
or social justice. This partly meets the need from which we

began just because the range of possible applications is determined by criteria supplied by the theory of social justice. Possible applications must be implementations of acceptable material principles, which tell us what are relevant differences and similarities for the purposes of discrimination. I followed Feinberg in saying that an 'acceptable' material principle was one which discriminated on characteristics the individuals had had a 'fair opportunity' to acquire or avoid. I argued that, despite first impressions, the test does allow positive discrimination which removes or compensates other discrimination as a matter of *justice*. I also described how positive discrimination to remove and compensate for 'natural' handicaps might be argued to be a matter of justice through its fostering *equality*.

9   Discrimination and social control

The suggestion that society may have a responsibility to foster equality warrants further discussion. I shall not offer such discussion yet; arguments for social policies recognising basic human needs or others assigning moral status to strangers as *fellow-men* all might play a part in such a discussion. We have already touched on these arguments in Part one, and will return to related arguments about human rights later in Part two. In the meantime we have other fish to fry.

Discrimination as to which merit or desert figures as a criterion yields a social policy which provides both care and control. Those possessing the meritorious characteristic(s) are to be treated alike and favourably. The undeserving are thus encouraged to acquire the meritorious characteristics and thus controlled. The more unfavourable their treatment, the greater the control.

I want now to focus on merit or desert as a material principle of social justice and to discuss the logical relations between moral relationships, social control and stigma.

The suggestion that our social services are instruments of social control is hardly novel. In what follows I shall

presume that the suggestion is true of selective services
where merit is in question, even if it is not all that can
be said. What I want to discuss next are recent attempts
to characterise the social morality implied by the control
exercised, through its allocation of stigma. I begin with
a discussion of 'the work ethic' and then argue its
limitations through a discussion of the residual and
institutional models of social welfare. I then give an
exposition of a more, and, perhaps, surprisingly adequate
ethic, 'respect for persons'. 'Respect for persons', I
shall argue, is more adequate than 'the work ethic' as a
source of justification for the allocation of stigma in our
social services, but its greater adequacy is a surprise,
because respectors of persons are usually not thought to soil
their hands in the allocation of stigma. I go on to suggest
that the 'caring professions' should abandon 'respect for
persons' for, although it provides a moral reason for social
control, through the allocation of stigma, to those not
exercising certain capacities, it provides little moral
reason for *care* of stigmatised individuals. I suggest the
direction in which we might seek principles providing greater
moral reason for care even in these cases.

It is perhaps worth saying at the outset that I offer no
definition of either 'status' or 'stigma'. Even so I would
say that I conceive of their relationship as symmetrical, and
would accept 'systematically structured social approval' as
an account of 'status' in this context, and 'systematically
structured social disapproval' as an account of 'stigma' in
this context. Arguing for amendment, the Poor Law Report of
1834 declared,

It appears to the pauper that the Government has undertaken
to repeal, in his favour, the ordinary laws of nature...

that no-one shall lose the means of comfortable
subsistence, whatever be his indolence, prodigality,;
or vice; in short, that the penalty which, after all, must
be paid by some one for idleness and improvidence, is
to fall, not on the guilty person or on his family,
but on the proprietors of the lands and houses
encumbered by his settlement (Checkland S.G. and E.O.,
1974, p.135).

Rather more recently, F. Fox Piven and R. Cloward have
argued that the

fundamental problem with which relief reform seeks to
cope is the erosion of the work role. When large
numbers of people come to subsist on the dole, many of
them spurning what little low-wage work may exist, those
of the poor and near-poor who continue to work are
inevitably affected. From their perspective, the ready
availability of relief payments (often at levels only
slightly below prevailing wages) undermines their chief
claim to social status: namely, that although poor they
nevertheless earn their livelihood (1971, p.343).

It doesn't follow from this analysis that one should
reduce relief payments or make them less readily available,
one might raise wages and create more jobs.

The point I want to extract from both the Poor Law Report
and Fox Piven and Cloward, is that both endorse what
Robert Pinker (1974) has called 'the work ethic': earning
one's livelihood is one's chief claim to social status; to
abandon the work role is, quite properly, to be subject to
stigma.

Pinker illustrates the work ethic as it is manifested in
current social policy in Britain, arguing that in general
The influence of the work ethic is most evident in income

maintenance services but it has also directly affected
the ordering of priorities in other social services such
as health and welfare.   Work and self-help are the best
means by which the good citizen ensures his independence
in health and adversity (1974, p.4).

Unemployment benefit and the disqualifications of the
wage-stop are the obvious example everyone has in mind.

Now, it seems to me that, as a characterisation of the
morality which would be invoked to justify the social
control exercised by social services involved in income
maintenance, the title is particularly appropriate, though
the account is as yet too brief.   *Why* should the work role
be one's chief claim to social status?

The Poor Law Report suggests that the explication of the
work ethic should proceed along utilitarian lines:

   although we admit that able-bodied persons in the receipt
   of out-door allowances and partial relief may be, and in
   some are, placed in a condition less eligible than that
   of the independent labourer of the lowest class.   ...The
   express or implied ground of his application is, that he is
   in danger of perishing from want.   Requesting to be rescued
   from that danger out of the property of others, he must
   accept assistance on the terms, whatever they may be,
   which the common welfare requires (Checkland, 1974, p.376).

So, presumably, the Poor Law (Amendment) act of 1834, which
according to Titmuss (1974) aimed 'to drive men to work or
into the workhouse', attached stigma to receipt of welfare
provision and status to the work role because this served
'the common welfare'.

Fox Piven and Cloward offer an explanation of the threat
to the common welfare:

   when attachments to the work role deteriorate, so do

attachments to the family, especially the attachment of
men to their families. For all practical purposes, the
relief check becomes a surrogate for the male breadwinner.
The resulting family breakdown and loss of control over
the young is usually signified by the spread of certain
forms of disorder - for example, school failure, crime
and addiction (1971, p. 343).

On this explanation, the common welfare is presumed to lie
in the *status quo* as regards family life, school attendance,
adherence to laws, and so on. Which is not to say that one
could not take a different view of 'the common welfare' and
continue to attach status to the work role.

However, though 'the work ethic' is an appropriate title
for the morality which could be invoked to justify the social
control exercised by social services involved in income
maintenance, it seems to me too narrow a conception to
characterise adequately the morality which might be invoked
to justify the social control exercised by merit-based,
selective social services as a whole. What I should like
to do next is draw attention to an account of a non-
utilitarian morality which will serve *this* purpose. Once
the account has been given, it should be clear that the
morality in question would attach status to the work role,
but its allocation of status and stigma is not merely a
matter of whether or not one adopts the work role. It
allocates status and stigma in other contexts, and for this
reason is more suitable in the justification of the social
control exercised by merit-based, selective social services
as a whole.

I should like to approach the morality in question *via*
comment on what Pinker has described as 'currently the two
most influential theoretical formulations in social policy'

(1970), that is the 'residual' and 'institutional'
conceptions of social welfare policy. A full account of
these two conceptions can be found in Wilensky and Lebeaux.
For the present, two quotations will suffice. On the
residual conception, the social welfare structure

is conceived as a residual agency, attending primarily
to emergency functions, and is expected to withdraw when
the regular social structure - the family and the economic
system - is again working properly. Because of its
residual, temporary, substitute characteristic, social
welfare thus conceived often carried the stigma of 'dole'
or 'charity' (Wilensky and Lebeaux, 1965, p.139).

On the institutional conception, in contrast, welfare
services are seen 'as normal "first line" functions of
modern industrial society' (p.138). Further, the
institutional view

implies no stigma, no emergency, no 'abnormalcy'.
...The complexity of modern life if recognised. The
inability of the individual to provide fully for himself,
or to meet all his needs in family and work settings,
is considered a 'normal' condition; and the helping
agencies achieve 'regular' institutional status (p.140).

On Wilensky and Lebeaux's account, we may distinguish
the two conceptions through their different relations to
scope for stigmatisation. On the residual conception,
benefiting from social services may often be stigmatising,
while on the institutional conception, scope for
stigmatisation is restricted: though stigma may attach to
excessive dependence on public provision, such dependence in
itself implies no stigma at all.

This difference can be better understood if we remember
that stigma is a form of *discrimination*, and where it is a

consequence of social policy, we may expect it to be related
to some account, accepted in that society, of what makes
discrimination just. As we saw, Joel Feinberg (1973)
suggests that *relevant* grounds for socially just
discrimination must pass what he calls the 'fair opportunity'
test. Grounds for discrimination between two individuals
must be such that each has a fair opportunity to acquire or
avoid them: so that each is *responsible* for his possession
of the meritorious or stigmatising characteristic. Men do
not have an opportunity to acquire or avoid, and so are not
responsible for possession of a high IQ, possession of this
characteristic is therefore no relevant ground for
discrimination in favour of, or against, an individual. And
the same goes for one's sex and pigmentation, amongst other
things.

   On Feinberg's test, for receipt of social welfare
provision to be *relevant* grounds for discrimination, for
discrimination to be just, the individual or group concerned
must have had a fair opportunity to acquire or avoid being
in receipt of such provision; more particularly, it may be
just for receipt of welfare provision to be stigmatising
only if the individual or group has had a fair opportunity
to avoid being in receipt of such provision. (1)

   This criterion suggests the following explanation of the
different relations of the residual and institutional
conceptions to stigmatisation. On the residual conception,
receipt of social welfare provision may often be stigmatising
because the recipient is sometimes responsible for the
preferred structures of supply breaking down: he may leave
his job or alienate members of his family. In addition, in
cases in which the recipient is not responsible for the
breakdown in the preferred structures of supply, in a society

operating with Feinberg's criterion, in cases in which we
are ignorant of the facts of an individual case, when we
feel uncharitable we can presume responsibility and stigmatise
some individuals who in fact are not responsible for their
dependence. On the institutional conception no stigma is
implied because 'the complexity of modern life is recognised'.
That is, either individual responsibility for dependence is
denied, or it is impossible to be *sure* of individual
responsibility for dependence, and uncertainty in this
context may yield compassion. There is a presumption of less
than complete responsibility.

Now, the residual conception is usually supposed to
embody 'the work ethic'. I think it does, but that our
examination of it has brought out that this ethic is part of
a wider conception of social justice. The stigma allocated
on this conception attaches not only to those responsible
for loss of the work role, but also to those responsible
for a breakdown in family relationships such that the
family is no longer a source of welfare. And, correspondingly, status attaches not only to the fulfilment of the
work role, but also to the maintenance of supportive family
relationships.

An example of the place of the family as a source of
welfare on this model might be drawn from the Social Work
(Scotland) Act, 1968, 32(2a). A child may be referred to a
Children's Hearing as 'beyond the control of the parent' even
in cases where the manifestation of this lack of control is
not further possible grounds, such as offences. The
implication is that child or parents, or both, are
responsible for a breakdown in supportive family relationships
and, even if the agency assures them that its aim is to help,
must suffer the stigma of referral, and any supervision the

the Hearing may impose (see Watson, 1976).

Again, we invest a great deal of provision in attempts to keep families together, drawing up 'at risk' registers and mobilising a wide range of resources, from Family Service Units to the R.S.S.P.C.C. And an implication of all this is that status attaches to supportive family relationships, and stigma to responsibility for their loss. Clients gain status from co-operating with support offered, and even more from achieving independence of such support while sustaining the family. Stigma comes from non-co-operation and responsibility for continued dependence.

Because of the importance of the family as a source of welfare within the residual model, and the place, therefore, of responsibility for its cohesion or disintegration, as a criterion for the allocation of status and stigma, 'the work ethic' is too narrow a characterisation of its moral justification. I should like to suggest 'respect for persons' as a more appropriate characterisation, and now proceed to one influential (see Central Council for Education and Training in Social Work, 1976, ch.3) account of that principle which I think distributes stigma and status in the required way. The suggestion is of interest because those working in the social services, social workers in particular, usually see themselves as respecters of persons and *therefore* opposed to stigma. In what follows I shall suggest that as respecters of persons in the sense to be outlined, they must also allocate stigma, and be committed to that element of social control which stigmatisation provides.

Incidentally, though 'the work ethic' and, as I shall argue, 'respect for persons' are most readily linked with the residual model, there is nothing in the account given of the institutional model which is inconsistent with them. The

institutional model denies, or denies that we can often
be sure of, individual responsibility for dependence, it does
not deny that were an individual clearly responsible for his
dependence, or for a degree of dependence, then he should be
stigmatised.

Downie and Telfer analyse the principle of respect for
persons using the notion of 'the distinctive endowment of a
human being'. The distinctive endowment of a human being,
and that which makes him worthy of respect and a *person* is
'the practical exercise of reason'. That is

The ability to choose for oneself, and, more extensively,
to formulate purposes, plans and policies of one's own.
A second and closely connected element is the ability to
carry out decisions, plans or policies without undue
reliance on the help of others (1969, p.20).

Given that this is an analysis of the practical *exercise*
of reason, the abilities mentioned in this analysis of what
it involves must also at some time be manifested by the
individual *actually carrying out* decisions, plans or policies
without undue reliance on the help of others, and so on.

If this analysis is correct, any individual unduly reliant
upon the help of others in carrying out decisions, plans or
policies is less worthy of respect, and perhaps not worthy
of respect at all. Of course, much turns on the answer to
the question 'what reliance on the help of others is due?'
In relation to the help of social services, the residual and
institutional models differ markedly on this point. On the
former model such help is not often due from others than one's
family or, say, one's employer, on the latter it is usually
due. At any rate, it should be clear that an individual
responsible for his dependence on social services to provide
what would otherwise be found through his fulfilment of the

work role or maintenance of supportive family relationships,
on the principle of respect for persons, is unduly reliant,
and the individual is justly a victim of stigma.

Respect for persons, as articulated by Downie and Telfer,
includes the work ethic, in stigmatising undue dependence
on social services through neglect of the work role, but
better characterises a moral justification for the allocation
of stigma on the residual model because in addition it
stigmatises responsibility for failure of the family to
supply welfare in appropriate circumstances. Those who
neglect their capacity and opportunity for self-help,
neglecting to adopt the work role or to sustain supportive
family relationships, fail to display those abilities which
make a human being worthy of respect. Stigma in such cases
is implied by respect for persons.

Given this analysis of what makes human beings worthy of
respect, and if Downie and Telfer are right in saying that
'the idea of the individual person as of supreme worth is
fundamental to the moral, political and religious ideals of
our society' (1969, p.9), then stigmatisation in such cases
is a demand of our social morality, and the residual model
must inevitably play an important part in our thinking about
use of social service provision.

The law is the most obvious instrument of social control,
but it is not the most pervasive. Social morality may lead
to the enactment and enforcement of certain laws, but it
allocates status and stigma more widely. Discussing 'the
fitting adjustment between individual independence and social
control', J.S. Mill (Warnock 1962, p.130) is very conscious
of the importance of social morality. He warns us 'against
the tendency of society to impose, by other means than civil
penalties, its own ideas and practices as rules of conduct on

those who dissent from them'. He declares

> Society can and does execute its own mandates: and if it
> issues wrong mandates instead of right, or any mandates
> at all in things with which it ought not to meddle, it
> practises a social tyranny more formidable than many kinds
> of political oppression, since, though not usually upheld
> by such extreme penalties, it leaves fewer means of
> escape, penetrating much more deeply into the details of
> life, enslaving the soul itself.

This last sentence stresses the importance of internalisation
of values, of self-discipline, to the control function of a
social morality.

So far in this chapter it has been my purpose to draw out
the relationship between a particular social morality and a
particular form of social control, by drawing attention to
its allocation of status and stigma. It seemed to me
important to show that respect for persons, as articulated
by Downie and Telfer, is a social morality which allocates
stigma to recipients of social welfare provision in the
specified circumstances, because the characterisation of the
social morality in question as 'the work ethic' is, I have
argued, too narrow. I should now like to turn to other
reasons.

The principle in this form is often espoused by 'the
caring professions' who, at the same time, claim to be
seeking 'ways and means, values, methods and techniques, of
positive discrimination without the infliction, actual or
imagined, or a sense of personal failure and individual
fault' (Titmuss, 1968, p.135. See also Pinker, 1970).

'Caring professions' seeking this goal will not find it
through 'respect for persons'. On this principle, as
articulated by Downie and Telfer, and which I have argued is

a moral basis for the residual model of welfare provision, the problem we face is not how to avoid stigmatising altogether, except in so far as misallocation stigmatises genuine 'social casualties' of our society, but how to ensure that stigma falls on irresponsible individuals. Indeed it seems to me that any social morality must presuppose some scope in social life for individual responsibility and irresponsibility, and so, on occasion, inflict a sense of personal failure and individual fault. That is, in so far as the allocation of stigma is governed by a social *morality*, with the necessary presumption of the capacity to choose being exercised by some individuals on some occasions, stigmatisation logically cannot be ruled out.

However, I said in my Introduction that I would conclude with the suggestion that the 'caring professions' abandon the principle of 'respect for persons'. Let me now explain why. If all social moralities entail scope for the allocation of stigma, the fact that 'respect for persons' does so will not provide us with a reason to abandon it in favour of any other principle. What does provide the 'caring professions' with a reason to abandon this principle in favour of another is the *narrow range* of characteristics it recognises as relevant in the allocation of status and stigma.

We may distinguish social moralities by the range of characteristics they recognise as status-enhancing and stigmatising; 'respect for persons' recognises only those capacities described earlier and brought together under the description 'the distinctive endowment of a human being' as relevant. As a result, a 'caring profession' adopting this principle must stigmatise individuals not exercising these capacities, though, so long as they are still possessed,

though not exercised, the profession has some moral reason
to care for these individuals: possession of the relevant
characteristics is status-enhancing, it tempers the stigma
attached to not exercising them, and leaves the individual
worthy of care as well as control.

However, given that the capacities which make up 'the
distinctive endowment of a human being', the ability to
choose for oneself, etc. are hardly possessed by very young
children and the senile, and not possessed at all by some
severely mentally handicapped individuals, 'respect for
persons' provides little and no moral reason, respectively,
for care of these individuals. We are only obliged to
control them. Caring professions working with these
individuals must find another principle if talk of 'caring'
is to be taken seriously.

Further, if we abandon 'respect for persons' in favour
of a social morality recognising a wider range of
characteristics as relevant in the allocation of status and
stigma, it is of course much more likely that the client,
even if lacking in some, will possess others of the valued
characteristics. The wider the range of characteristics
our social morality recognises as relevant, the more
individuals we have some moral reason to care for. If our
client possesses the capacities of a *person*, we have one
moral reason; if he possesses this distinctive endowment of
a human being and other valued capacities, we have more than
one moral reason to care. And if our other valued characteristics include some possessed by the severely mentally
handicapped, we have moral reason to care for clients whom
mere respecters of persons have no moral reason to help.

It has been suggested to me by Robert Pinker, in discussion
of these points, that in the last analysis it would be

sufficient to settle for compassion for such 'non-persons',
whether or not they are worthy of our care, in order to keep
them from extreme destitution and distress. However, I don't
think this is sufficient simply because such compassion
requires principled grounding. As I have argued elsewhere
(Watson, 1978), there is a logical connection between
attitudes and principles of action: if a person has a certain
attitude towards something, he will necessarily adopt certain
principles of action towards it. And as I have argued in
the same place, the attitude of compassion, where such human
beings are the objects of that attitude, entails adopting
a principle of respect for human beings and not respect for
persons. Compassion *alone* cannot be sufficient for care
of such individuals because such compassion entails adopting
a moral principle recognising them as worthy of care in
virtue of their possession of certain valued characteristics,
characteristics *other than* those distinctive of a person.

Social moralities which recognise a wider range of
characteristics as relevant in the allocation of status and
stigma might, I suggest, be labelled forms of 'respect for
human beings'. Any principle called 'respect for human
beings', then, will recognise a wider range of relevant
characteristics, but some forms, of course, will recognise
a wider range than others as relevant. It is for the 'caring
professions' to consider how wide a range they regard as
relevant in the allocation of status and stigma. Let me
simply offer an example of one form of 'respect for human
beings' and illustrate a corollary. Our 'respect for human
beings' might entail valuing the capacity to be emotionally
secure, the desire to give and the capacity to receive love
and affection, as well as the distinctive endowment of a
human being. Take the case of a man sacked because of his

absenteeism due to his desire to spend more time caring for
his children. Our principle confers status for the desire
to give love and affection while conferring stigma for undue
reliance on the help of others. Or again in the case of a
child truanting persistently to stay at home in a close-knit
loving family, our principle confers status for the desire
to give and the capacity to receive love and affection, as
well as stigma for refusal to develop one's distinctive
endowment as a human being (assuming school attendance helps
in this). In all cases, the wider the range of characteristics relevant to allocation of status and stigma, though
the client is subject to social control, he is also more
likely to be worthy of care (see Watson 1978, ch.2).

Of course I am not suggesting that changes in the
structure of social approval and disapproval in our society,
particularly as manifested in the work of the 'caring
professions', are easily achieved. But deliberate and
morally justifiable modification of that structure is
possible only if we have identified the structures entailed
by different social moralities. These social moralities,
and their constituent moral principles, in allocation of
the status and stigma they entail, determine the balance and
distribution of care and control.

Let me draw this particular discussion to a close by
summarising the points which are relevant to our thinking
about merit or desert as a criterion of just discrimination.
We followed Feinberg in saying that status or stigma may
justly attach to an individual only if he is responsible for
his possession of the meritorious or stigmatising characteristic. 'The work ethic' makes earning one's livelihood a
meritorious characteristic, though we may remain worthy of
care without it, provided we are not responsible for our

unemployment.   'Respect for persons' makes 'the practical
exercise of reason' meritorious, but again we may remain
worthy of care, provided we are not responsible for its
loss.   In each case, without the meritorious characteristic
we may remain worthy of care provided we retain the *capacity*
to earn our livelihood or engage in the practical exercise
of reason, respectively, and would do so were it not for
circumstances beyond our control.   But some individuals
do not possess these capacities.   If we are to justify
caring for them as a matter of *merit*, other characteristics
which they do possess must be admitted as meritorious.
Forms of 'respect for human beings' help in this manner, and
not only justify social policies aiming to help such
incapable individuals who are responsible for their loss of
employment and failure to engage in the practical exercise
of reason.

Forms of 'respect for human beings' broaden the range of
characteristics regarded as meritorious, and thus allow more
individuals to be recognised as worthy of care. We may go
further and recognise all individuals as worthy of care if
we recognise a sufficiently wide range of characteristics
as meritorious. Alternatively, and only apparently more
simply (see Feinberg, 1973, ch.6), we may recognise *being
human* as itself meritorious, though this will never be
useful in justifying *discrimination* among men, however
positive. Merit is usually a matter of being an outstanding
member of a class and thus characteristics of all members
(indeed the classifying characteristics) are not a sign of
merit.

But perhaps respect for human beings, caring for strangers,
can be more satisfactorily grounded not in merit but in
common human needs. In Part one, Chapter 4, speaking of our
moral obligations to strangers, I said that if we know the
strangers to be human, we have certain moral duties towards
them and they have corresponding rights. And this is
because, knowing them to be human, we know they have certain
basic needs. This line of thought is not without its
difficulties. Why ought we to try to meet basic or other

common human needs?   I shall not now try to answer this
question, though I think we might begin by saying that if we
ought to do anything we ought at least to do this.   However
we enlarge upon the claim that their being human justifies
caring for strangers, we shall be developing a conception
of our moral relationship to strangers as our fellow-men,
which recognises our obligations to them as fellow-men, and
their corresponding *human rights*.   I want now to introduce
the idea of human rights through discussion of its place in
a welfare rights approach to social service policies.

It has long been recognised that social work is at least
in part regulated by moral principles.   Textbooks (Biestek,
1961; Moffett, 1968) regularly list such things as
individualisation, acceptance and self-determination as
casework values, professional bodies generate codes of ethics
for social work (British Association of Social Workers, 1973),
and teachers of social administration 'attempt a clarification
of the moral ideals of social welfare' (Pinker, 1974).

The importance of moral principles has continued to be
stressed in the development of a 'welfare rights' approach
in social work.   Moral principles held relevant to casework
are not abandoned, but at the same time there is evidence
in social work literature of a new emphasis.   Rosalind Brooke
(1972) argues that if we are to pursue a welfare rights
approach 'we need some framework within which to examine
rights within the social services'.   Brooke suggests that
'one useful frame of reference can be found within certain
articles of the European Convention on Human Rights' and goes
on in her essay to employ this framework in just such an
examination.   Wayne Vasey (1970) and R.G. Walton (1975) have
also recently stressed the importance of human rights as
goals for a welfare rights approach because of their relation

to our idea of social justice: a just society guarantees
human rights.

Both Vasey and Walton have in mind human rights as listed
in the United Nations Universal Declaration of Human Rights,
proclaimed in 1948. (1)   Brooke, as I have said, recommends
the European Convention.   Does it matter which we choose?
I think it does, and for the following reasons.

We may draw a broad distinction between 'civil and
political' rights and 'social and economic' rights.   The
rights to life, freedom of movement and freedom of opinion
fall into the first class, the rights to work and to social
security fall into the second class.   The European Convention
concentrates primarily, though not exclusively, (2) on civil
and political rights.   Brooke quotes article 6(1) which
begins, 'In the determination of his civil rights and
obligations or of any criminal charge against him, everyone
is entitled to a fair and public hearing within a reasonable
time by an independent and impartial tribunal established
by law'.   Such civil and political rights have an important
place in a welfare rights approach.   In this case, as Brooke
points out (1972, p.248), we are led to ask whether particular
services are being fairly administered, whether the
recipient is being given adequate notice of a hearing to
curtail his benefit, whether reputable evidence is being
used as a basis for allocating or curtailing benefit, and
so on.

Even so, I think we should choose the Universal
Declaration rather than the European Convention as the
framework for a welfare rights approach to social work.   All
the civil and political rights proclaimed in the European
Convention are included in the Universal Declaration but the
latter also includes additional social and economic rights.

No framework for a welfare rights approach in social work
could be adequate if it did not, for example, recognise
that

Everyone has the right to a standard of living adequate
for the health and well-being of himself and his family,
including food, clothing, housing and medical care and
necessary social services, and the right to security in
the event of unemployment, sickness, disability,
widowhood, old age or other lack of livelihood in
circumstances beyond his control

or that 'Everyone has the right to rest and leisure,
including reasonable limitation of working hours and periodic
holidays with pay', (articles 25(1) and 24 respectively of
the Universal Declaration). As Wayne Vasey put it, 'The
Universal Declaration included economic, social, and
cultural, as well as political and civil, rights. Who more
than the people engaged in social welfare should recognise
the validity of this scope of rights?' (1970, p.84).

If human rights are to provide a framework within which
to examine rights within the social services, our list of
human rights must include social and economic rights as well
as civil and political rights, and the Universal Declaration
seems the obvious choice. However, objections have recently
been raised even to the *possibility* of a framework proclaiming
such a range of human rights. Professor Maurice Cranston
has recently put forward philosophical and political
objections to the classification of certain social and
economic rights, including those proclaimed in articles 24
and 25(1) of the Universal Declaration quoted earlier, as
human rights. Cranston sets out three 'tests for the
authenticity of a human right' (3) which though passed by
the traditional civil and political rights, he argues, the

social and economic rights in question fail. Cranston
uses the tests to distinguish rights in these two classes.
Only the civil and political rights pass these tests, so only
they are human rights. This philosophical criticism of the
Universal Declaration is backed by a political point: 'The
circulation of a confused notion of human rights hinders
the effective protection of what are correctly seen as human
rights.' (1967, p.43)

Brooke chooses not to discuss 'the philosophical basis of
rights' (1972, p.248) but, faced by a philosophical objection
to a framework which includes social and economic rights, if
we wish to employ such a framework we *must* enter into the
philosophical debate. We might avoid this terrible fate by
denying the value of employing such a framework, but I
don't think anyone seriously concerned with a welfare rights
approach in social work would offer such a denial. The
aim of the approach is legal recognition of welfare rights.
Since, as Cranston puts it, 'a human right is something of
which no one may be deprived without a grave affront to
justice' (1967, p.42), the framework in question provides
us with a strong moral argument which may be deployed in
defending and extending legal entitlement to welfare rights.

I turn, then, to the philosophical debate. If I can show
that the social and economic rights in question pass
Cranston's three 'tests for the authenticity of a human
right', the Universal Declaration is released as a framework
for a welfare rights approach.

Cranston's three tests test practicability, paramount
importance and universality. As we shall see, the first
test is presented in a way which suggests that it must be
passed if what is claimed is to be a right of any kind,
unlike the second and third tests, which are tests of being

a *human* right. Further, since Cranston concludes in the
case of *each* test that a certain right does not qualify as a
human right simply because it fails that test, it seems that
each test provides a *necessary* condition for being a human
right. That is, any right purporting to be a human right
must pass all three of these tests.

Rights bear a clear relationship to duties [says Cranston,]
and the first test of both is that of practicability. It
is not my duty to do what it is physically impossible
for me to do. You cannot reasonably say it was my duty
to have jumped into the Thames at Richmond to rescue a
drowning child if I was nowhere near Richmond at the time
the child was drowning. What is true of duties is
equally true of rights. If it is impossible for a thing
to be done, it is absurd to claim it as a right. At
present it is utterly impossible, and will be for a long
time yet, to provide 'holidays with pay' for everybody
in the world... The government of India, for example,
simply cannot command the resources that would guarantee
each one of the 480 million inhabitants of India 'a
standard of living adequate for the health and well-being
of himself and his family', let alone 'holidays with
pay', (pp.50-1).

In Cranston's example of the drowning child it *is*
impossible for me to rescue the child and, therefore, I cannot
be said to have a duty to do so. Given the correspondence
which rights bear to duties, in this case the child
correspondingly cannot be said to have a right against me to
be rescued. It is worth noting, however, that in Cranston's
example the impossibility is a *logical* impossibility. Given
the employment of spatio-temporal criteria in the
identification of particular people, it is logically

impossible for the same person to be in different places at
the same time. Given the employment of these criteria it is
inconceivable that I might at one and the same time be *both*
'nowhere near Richmond at the time the child was drowning'
and jumping in the Thames at Richmond to rescue him. It is
worth noting this feature of the example because it is a
serious weakness. If only the logically impossible fails
the test of practicability, then the social and economic
rights in question *pass* the test. We can certainly *conceive*
of everybody in the world being guaranteed 'a standard of
living adequate for the health and well-being of himself
and his family' and 'holidays with pay'.

However, this weakness is built into the test by mistake.
This is shown in Cranston's account of the test when he
says 'It is not my duty to do what it is *physically*
impossible for me to do' (italics mine) and '*At present* it
is utterly impossible, and *will be for* a long time yet, to
provide...' (italics mine). A logical impossibility does
not become a possibility *in time.* It is not Cranston's
view, then, that all logical possibilities pass the test of
practicability, but only those it is *at present* possible
to realise; it is these possibilities which generate
significant claims to rights. This is confirmed when he
later says 'A right...is something that can, and from the
moral point of view *must*, be respected here and now' (p.53).

It seems to me that a test of practicability which is
passed only by claims it is at present possible to realise,
is a reasonable test. But Cranston would add a further
qualification which prevents all such claims qualifying.
When he says 'The government of India, for example, simply
cannot command the resources that would guarantee each one
of the 480 million inhabitants of India ' a standard of

living adequate for the health and well-being of himself
and his family', Cranston implies that what is claimed is
a right *of* all men, but not necessarily *against* all men;
in the case in question, the right is implied to be a right
only against other inhabitants of India. Cranston's test of
practicability, then, is passed only by claims which every
state may at present satisfy for *its own* inhabitants.
Naturally, the social and economic rights in question fail
this test.

There seems no good reason why we should accept so tough
a test of practicability, why we should accept that the
social and economic rights in question should not be claimed
by all men *against* all men. Further, in setting such a test
Cranston is inconsistent with a position which he later
expounds (in Raphael, ed., 1967, p.96). He adopts a
distinction between rights of all men against all men and
rights of all men but not necessarily against all men,
allowing only the former to be classed as human rights. If
his test of practicability is to discover human rights, he
should surely pass as human rights all which are practicable
as rights claimed by all men *against all men,* and to be
consistent with his later view, he must.

If the social and economic rights in question are claimed
against all men, it is plausible to suggest (and I take the
United Nations Declaration to assume) that it *is* at present
possible to guarantee the new social and economic rights to
everybody in the world, and so significantly claim them as
human rights. As claims of all men against all men, the new
social and economic rights *pass* the test of practicability.

According to Professor David Raphael (Raphael, 1967,
pp.65-6),

When the Universal Declaration says that every man has the

right to work, or the right to subsistence, it does not
imply that the corresponding responsibility to provide
any particular man with work or subsistence rests on every
other man or every group of men; it implies that this
responsibility rests on the members of his own State, and
that the government of that State has a duty to carry
out the responsibility on behalf of all its members. We
do of course speak of a responsibility to help people who
are in need in other parts of the world, but such help
is an act of benevolence or charity, nor a matter of
implementing a right.

I see no reason to accept either of these statements
and Raphael offers no arguments in their support. Of course,
it may be admitted that a social or economic right of all men
against all men *would* fail the test of practicability if it
implied that a *personal* responsibility to provide any
particular man with work or subsistence, or whatever, rests
on every other man; it is of course not possible at present
for every other man, independently of every other man, to
provide these things. On the other hand if this were implied
in the test of practicability, the *traditional* human rights
to life, liberty and a fair trial would also fail. It is
not possible at present for every other man independently
to guarantee these rights for any particular man. However,
a right of all men against all men does *not* fail the test
of practicability if what is implied is that a responsibility
to provide what is claimed rests on all men collectively
rather than singly, since I believe it is possible at present
for all men collectively to provide these things. I conclude
from this discussion, then, that as claims of all men
against all men collectively, the new social and economic
rights *pass* the test of practicability.

This assumes of course that *as a matter of fact* at
present all men collectively possess adequate natural
resources, and administrative ingenuity, to guarantee these
rights to all men. At various times it may not be possible
to guarantee the new social and economic rights in full,
but surely men are able to guarantee the new rights *in part*.
As Raphael says

> a sort of system of social security is to be found in the
> Old Testament laws about leaving harvest gleanings for
> the poor, the periodic cancellation of debts, and so
> forth. Again, while unemployment is among the greatest
> of evils for those who are subject to it, no amount of
> reading Lord Keynes will produce a golden key for full
> employment everywhere, yet there is some possibility
> nowadays of some control of unemployment by governments,
> as there was not in former times... (1967, pp.63-4)

and therefore it is justifiable to speak of a duty to do
what we can, and a right that it be done. If Cranston holds
that rights which, at present, it is possible to guarantee
only *in part* fail the test of practicability for human rights,
then social and economic rights may fail to qualify as
human rights, but so do such traditional rights as the rights
to life, liberty and a fair trial, which he wants to say
are human rights. As Raphael points out 'no amount of
criminal legislation or of police forces will be able to
prevent *all* homicides; but that is no reason for saying that
the right to life should be struck out of our list of human
rights as not being universally practicable' (1967, p.64).
If practicability requires the possibility of at present
meeting obligations *in full*, then Cranston applies this test
inconsistently; if practicability requires only the
possibility of at present meeting obligations *in part*,

then both the new social and economic rights and the
traditional civil and political rights are practicable: the
test of practicability provides no ground for denying that
the social and economic rights in question are human rights.

There are two further points I should like to make
about the test of practicability in the revised form which
I accept. First, I would use the test to discriminate
between rights and ideals. But then, it may be objected,
even in its revised form the test is too easily a defence
of the *status quo*. Reforms which take a year or more will
be not 'at present possible', will be classed as ideals,
and thus filed away and forgotten. Cranston too has this
view of ideals. In reply I would simply point out that it
does not follow from the fact that we do not expect ideals
to be fulfilled at present, that we do not expect a
government, say, to take all necessary steps for their
fulfilment as soon as possible. Though not at present
possible, an ideal is precisely something that is *pursued*
and not forgotten.

Second, I should make the point that as a way of
discriminating between rights and ideals, the test of
practicability draws no sharp boundaries. 'At present' is
clearly vague, and, I think, usefully so, leaving room for
some debate about what can be done, what claims can at
present be satisfied.

Next the test of *paramount importance*. 'Here the
distinction' between human rights and social and economic
rights, says Cranston,

is less definite, but no less crucial. And here again
there is a parallel between rights and duties. It is a
paramount duty to relieve great distress, as it is not a
paramount duty to give pleasure. It would have been my

duty to rescue the drowning child at Richmond if I had
been there at the time; but it is not, in the same sense,
my duty to give Christmas presents to the children of my
neighbours.... Common sense knows that fire engines and
ambulances are essential services, whereas fun fairs and
holiday camps are not (p.51).

Cranston then suggests that 'ordinary people find themselves
invoking the language of human rights' in defence of the
traditional human rights, say where there is an invasion of
the human right to freedom of movement. 'In considering
cases of this kind,' he says, 'we are confronted by matters
which belong to a totally different moral dimension from
questions of social security and holidays with pay. A human
right is something of which no-one may be deprived without
a grave affront to justice' (p.52).

This discussion seems to me quite unsuccessful. Cranston
admits that there is a paramount *duty* to relieve great
distress; given the correspondence between rights and duties
which he again emphasises, there must then surely be a
paramount *right* to the relief of great distress. Or rather
there must be a group of paramount rights each to the relief
of a different form of great distress, and including, surely,
paramount rights to the relief of great social and economic
distresses. Cranston can avoid this conclusion only if he
denies that social and economic distresses are great
distresses. This, in effect, he does in saying that a human
right, but not a social or economic right, 'is something of
which no-one may be deprived without a grave affront to
justice' 9p.52). The denial is implausible.

Raphael presses this point when he says
Tom Paine evidently understood the natural right to life
as implying not only laws against homicide but also laws

to provide a bare subsistence. Will anyone say that he was
wrong in terms of paramount importance?   Importance, like
practicability, is of course a matter of degree, and no
doubt the prevention of murder is of more paramount [sic]
importance than the prevention of starvation.   Yet the
degrees of paramountcy do not place all the rights of
liberty before all the economic and social rights.   If a
man is subject to chronic unemployment in a depressed
area, he will not thank you for the information that he
.has the basic rights of liberty (1967, p.63).

We may conclude that the test of paramount importance
does not in general distinguish traditional human rights
from the social and economic rights in question, nor does it,
then, provide grounds for denying that the welfare rights
which these include are human rights.

Next, the test of genuine *universality*.   'This' says
Cranston,

the so-called human right to holidays with pay plainly
cannot pass.   For it is a right that is necessarily
limited to those persons who are *paid* in any case, that is
to say, to the *employé* class.   Since not everyone belongs
to this class, the right cannot be a universal right, a
right which, in the terminology of the Universal
Declaration, 'everyone' has.   That the right to a holiday
with pay is for many people a real moral right, I would
not for one moment deny.   But is it a right which...can
be claimed by members of a specific class of persons
because they are members of that class' (p.51)

Cranston would no doubt raise the same objection to a claim
to a social (welfare) right to unemployment benefit as a human
right.   Since not everyone belongs to the class of the
unemployed, the right cannot be a universal right, it is

rather a right which can be claimed by members of a specific
class of persons *because* they are members of that class.

In parallel with Cranston's argument we might say 'this
so-called human right to a fair trial plainly cannot pass
the test of universality. For it is a right that is
necessarily limited to those persons who are *on trial* in
any case, that is to say the *accusé* class; since not everyone
belongs to this class, the right cannot be a universal right,
a right which "everyone" has; it is rather a right which
can be claimed by members of a specific class of persons
because they are members of that class.' By the same form of
argument the traditional rights to leave any country,
including one's own, to freedom of religion and freedom of
peaceful assembly, are excluded from the class of human
rights, since each is 'necessarily limited' to those persons
who are leaving a country, religious, and peacefully
assembling, respectively.

Indeed, it is difficult to think of any of the traditional
civil and political rights which satisfy this test of
universality. It is not true that everyone's life, liberty
or security of person is threatened and so it is not true
that everyone is now in circumstances appropriate to the
exercise of these rights, and so they are not universal
rights. Cranston cannot be happy with this consequence. He
makes it quite clear at the beginning of his paper that his
objective is the effective protection of the traditional
human rights: 'The traditional human rights are political
and civil rights such as the right to life, liberty, and a
fair trial' (p.43). It is a consequence of his own
application of the test of universality that precisely these
rights are not universal rights and so are not due the
effective protection due to human rights!

Thus applied, the test of universality fails to distinguish between traditional human rights and the social and economic rights in question. If this test, thus applied, supplied Cranston's ground for denying that social and economic rights are human rights, he must apply it inconsistently. On the other hand, it seems clear that the test is misapplied. The test is a test of whether or not everyone has the right, but we pass only rights which everyone is now in appropriate circumstances to exercise. As a result the rights to periodic holidays with pay and to a fair trial, and the others, are not universal rights. It is time to start again.

The test of universality is passed by rights which everyone has. Cranston argues that the right to periodic holidays with pay (and, no doubt, others of the social and economic rights in question) is not a right which everyone has, because it is a right which 'can be claimed by members of a specific class of persons *because* they are members of that class' (where 'a specific class' is less than all men). The force of this description is to suggest that the rights in question are rights of the kind attached to a *social role*. We may, for example, say of the right of a father to discipline his child, that he can claim it just because he is a member of a specific class of persons: he is a father. Such rights are not universal, and are not *human* rights.

But what of the rights of those in employment? Is 'being employed' a social role? There are many types of employment, each itself a social role; each constituted by its own set of rights and duties; teacher, cook, carpenter, barman, and so on. Can all these different roles be said to be part of one role - being employed - to which attach a set of rights?

We might be led to think that this is so by suggested examples of such rights, suggestions such as 'the right to

periodic holidays with pay', 'the right to reasonable
limitation of working hours', and so on. But I think that,
in these cases at least, we would have been, and Cranston
is, *mis*led. This emerges in the form of justification
offered. A man's right to discipline his child would be
justified by saying 'he is a father'. The same form of
justification does not suffice in these other cases.

Why should that man enjoy reasonable limitation of his
working hours? Because he is in employment. This reply
simply won't do as a justification. To be a father is,
amongst other things, to have the right to discipline your
children. But to be in employment entails nothing about
the limitation of your working hours. The reply we need,
I suggest, is 'Because he is an employed *man*'. We justify
a reasonable limitation of working hours by referring not to
the fact that the man is employed, but to the fact that he is
a *human being*. This is true of the right to periodic
holidays with pay, and it is even more obviously true of
the right to a fair trial: Why should that man be given a
fair trial? Because he is accused? No, because he is an
accused *man*.

We *may* say that the social and economic rights in question,
and the civil and political rights mentioned in my parallel
argument, 'can be claimed by members of a specific class of
persons *because* they are members of that class'. But we
must *beware* of saying that therefore they are not rights
which 'everyone' has. This again is to presume 'being
employed', 'being on trial' 'being religious', and so on,
to be social roles. Certainly, in the case of rights attached
to social roles, we can identify all the possessors of the
rights as all those in that role. Every father, and no one
else, has the distinctive rights of a father. This is not

true for rights justified *not* by reference to the social
role of the claimant, but by reference to his humanity. To
say that a man possesses a right to a fair trial just because
he is a human being implies that he possessed that right
before being accused. Rights justified by reference to being
human are rights possessed before becoming a member of any
specific class of persons (and they are retained).

If we say that such rights 'can be claimed by members of a
specific class of persons *because* they are members of that
class', this must simply express the point that these are
rights which can be exercised only when one is in a certain
situation, a situation which not everyone is in. Only a man
on trial can exercise his right to a fair trial; and not
everyone is on trial. But *anyone* might be in a situation in
which these rights can be exercised. They therefore remain
rights which *everyone* has. They may be rights 'necessarily
limited' to members of a specific class of persons, in the
sense that only certain people are in the situation in which
these rights can be exercised, but they are, nevertheless,
rights *possessed* by all men.

Cranston demands of a universal right that everyone must
belong to the class of people for whom it is an occasion
appropriate to its exercise; I have sketched some consequences
of this demand. Recognising that one may be a possessor
of a right without being a person for whom it is an occasion
appropriate to its exercise, we can alternatively demand of
a universal right only that everyone possess it simply by
virtue of being human.

This demand retains the distinction between rights which
are universal and rights which are not; the right not to be
held in slavery or servitude is, on this test, a universal
right, the right of arrest is not. The right of arrest is

justified by reference to satisfaction of further conditions
than simply being human, such as, say, being a member of the
police forces. Further, the traditional civil and political
rights to life, liberty, a fair trial, and so on are also
universal rights; they are rights possessed simply by virtue
of being human. However, on this test the social and
economic rights in question are also universal rights; these
too are possessed simply by virtue of being human. The
Universal Declaration says that human rights are validated
by reference to the 'inherent dignity...of all members of
the human family'. It seems to me that this form of
justification is available equally to the civil and
political and the social and economic rights in question.
The rights to reasonable limitation of working hours and to
periodic holidays with pay, though exercisable only on
specific types of occasion are possessed, and may be
exercised on such occasions, by everyone, it may plausibly
be argued, simply by virtue of being human; such rights
recognise the inherent dignity of man.

If this is correct, the revised test of universality
fails to supply grounds for denying that the social and
economic rights in question are human rights.

The adjustment I have proposed for the test of universality
is particularly relevant to welfare rights. Over recent
years there has been, and indeed there still is, a debate
about whether social welfare services should be universal
or selective. One might assume that services labelled
'universal', like health and education, pass the test of
universality; one might also assume that services labelled
'selective' do not pass this test. *Selective* services
provide benefits to people who 'fit into a number of common
categories of need, by virtue of sickness, old age or

unemployment'. (4)   It is therefore important to notice that
much selective as well as universal provision corresponds to
rights which *pass* the test of universality; 'concentrating
help on those whose needs are greatest' does not prevent our
claiming the welfare rights in question as human rights. The
welfare rights corresponding to selective services are
usually rights which may be exercised only on specific
types of occasion - in sickness, old age or unemployment,
say, but we may still claim that they are social rights
which are possessed and may be exercised on the appropriate
occasion by all men. The claim that they are human rights is
not undermined even if it is true that as a matter of fact
not all men are in the circumstances which qualify one for
the benefit or service in question, since any man might be,
and would be entitled simply by virtue of being human; the
test of universality is passed.

Much selective treatment is like this, but not all. We
may all hope or expect to live to old age and draw our old
age pensions, but, since a large part of our population is
not female, we cannot plausibly claim that a right to a
widow's pension is possessed and may be exercised by all
mankind on the appropriate occasion. Entitlement is not
simply by virtue of being human. Such rights thus fail the
revised test of universality, though even in these cases
being human is a necessary condition of possession. At
least, such rights fail the revised test of universality
when they are thus specified. Welfare rights may express
human rights in a particular historical and social setting,
and rights such as that to a widow's pension may be seen as
the human right to 'a standard of living adequate for the
health and well-being of himself and his family' expressed
in relation to bereaved women in a certain society. At

different times different groups will need attention drawn
to their possession of certain human rights and this may
result in legislation recognising rights which refer only to
the endangered group, as in this case. Such welfare rights
are not human rights on the revised test of universality,
but they may be supported by reference to human rights since
they defend the human rights of a particular group. The
human rights framework is again useful.

It is my conclusion, then, that the three tests of
practicability, paramount importance and universality,
though appropriate types of test, quite fail to provide
grounds for distinguishing the social and economic rights
from the civil and political rights in question, and fail
to provide grounds for denying that the welfare rights
included in the former are human rights. The tests are:

1 To pass the test of practicability it must at present
be possible for all men collectively to guarantee all men
the right in question, at least in part.

2 To pass the test of paramount importance the right
in question must be one of which no one may be deprived
without a grave affront to justice.

3 To pass the test of universality the right in question
must be possessed by all men simply by virtue of being
human.

It might be admitted that Cranston's tests, even in their
revised forms, fail to supply *philosophical* grounds for
placing social and economic, and civil and political rights
in different categories. Nevertheless, it might be said,
there is still *political* point in holding the two groups
apart. It will be recalled that I said earlier that Cranston
raised political as well as philosophical dounts about
including social and economic rights in a list of human

rights, and both may not fall to the same philosophical
arguments: though I may have released the Universal
Declaration from philosophical objections to its use as a
framework for a welfare rights approach in social work, it
may still be that use of this framework is impolitic. Towards
the end of his paper Cranston says that if the social and
economic rights in question are also proclaimed as human
rights,

> the effect may even be to bring the whole concept of
> human rights into disrepute. 'It would be a splendid
> thing', people might say, 'for everyone to have holidays
> with pay, a splendid thing for everyone to have social
> security, a splendid thing to have equality before the
> law, and freedom of speech, and the right to life. One
> day, perhaps, this beautiful ideal may be realized...'
> (p.52).

Cranston is here drawing the distinction between rights
and ideals. Even if one admitted that the social and
economic rights in question passed the revised test of
practicability and were rights rather than ideals, one might
be tempted to suggest that social and economic rights are
more like ideals than are civil and political rights. And
in that case one would think it politic to keep the two
groups of human rights apart - for the effective protection
of the civil and political rights. One might be so tempted if
one thought of civil rights as 'designed to guarantee the
individual against arbitrary treatment', and political rights
as 'designed to relate the government to the consent of the
governed', but social and economic rights as 'rights which
require that something be done if they are to be secured for
their recipients' (McKeon, 1949). On this view civil and
political rights are presented as implying only that a

negative obligation falls upon others, an obligation not to
interfere with your exercise of these rights; the social and
economic rights, on the other hand, place a *positive*
obligation upon others. A positive obligation is more
difficult to fulfil than a negative obligation, social and
economic rights are thus closer to (distant) ideals than
civil and political rights, and, for the effective
protection of the latter, should be kept distinct in practice
even if they are not significantly distinct in theory.

To use a disreputable phrase, I think that on reflection
this objection is seen to be ill-founded. First, one can
certainly think of cases in which great strength of will
is required if the exercise of civil and political rights
is not to be interfered with. A Ugandan government faced
with a popular demand for the expulsion of, or civil and
political discrimination against, Asians, would require
great strength of political will not to meet that demand.
Similarly someone witnessing the eviction of a family might
find self-restraint very difficult even supposing the
landlord to be acting within his civil rights. And one can
correspondingly think of cases in which very little strength
of will is required for something positive to be done to
secure a social or economic right. A British government or
whatever is one's own government, one might imagine, would
require little strength of political will to provide a man
suffering from long-term unemployment with subsistence.

Second, the distinction between rights to which negative
obligations correspond and rights to which positive
obligations correspond, is not parallel to that between civil
and political rights, on the one hand, and social and
economic rights, on the other. As Raphael notes,

when we say, for example, that a man has the right to

participate in government, we mean that those who
organize the political life of the country are obliged
to give him the opportunity to vote and make his opinions
known, and that they are further obliged to have regard
to his opinions when they take their political decisions
(1967, p.61).

Thus, to this *political* right there corresponds a *positive*
obligation which falls upon others.

Further, the courts, legislature, police force, defence
services and administrative services involved in government
do not compare all that favourably in terms of expense and
effort with provision for the social and economic rights in
question. In these terms social and economic rights in
general seem no closer to ideals than civil and political
rights.

A different political argument for keeping the two
groups of rights apart is offered by those who argue that
because the social and economic rights are 'rights which
require that something be done if they are to be secured
for their recipients', the promulgation of these rights has
'brought them into conflict with civil and political rights,
for the planning and control essential to the former impinge
on some of the freedom of choice and action that had seemed
defensible under the latter' (McKeon, p.44).

Two points might be made in reply. First, such conflict
can arise even between rights within just one of these
groups. For example, a man with a potentially fatal allergy
to raw meat might have his right to life secured by having his
right to freedom of movement diminished in the vicinity of
butcher's shops.

Second, although rights in the two groups sometimes
conflict, they also must often *co-operate*. This objection

and Cranston's discussion, of course, assume that the
traditional civil and political human rights can be secured
quite independently of the social and economic rights now
claimed. This assumption may be challenged. I earlier
quoted Raphael as saying that 'if a man is subject to chronic
unemployment in a depressed area, he will not thank you for
the information that he has the basic rights of liberty'. I
would suggest that such a man should not thank you, not
because what he lacks is equally as important as or more
important than liberty, but because his liberty is seriously
at risk if he does not enjoy certain social and economic
rights. In general, as Luc Somerhausen has put it,
'traditional human rights will not become a reality until
they have been completed by a social organisation which
makes it possible for man to protect himself against
exploitation' (1949, p.32). According to R.H. Tawney this
co-operation is even more extensive: 'political rights
afford a safeguard and significance to civil rights...
economic and social rights provide means essential to the
exercise of political rights...rights of communication and
thought may prepare the resolution of differences concerning
economic and social rights' (1937).

Article 3 of the Declaration proclaims the right to life.
As Raphael notes, life is not secured merely by ensuring
that no one takes it. Means of subsistence must be available,
the usual means being employment or unemployment benefit.
Article 7 says 'all are equal before the law and are entitled
without any discrimination to equal protection of the law'.
If the means to this protection is to be bought from lawyers,
the wherewithal must be available as of right to all - there
must be some scheme for legal aid. The right to freedom of
opinion and expression declared in Article 19 is secured

only if education, and indeed a certain kind of education, is available.

The assumption which seems to underly the view that the traditional civil and political human rights can be secured quite independently of the social and economic rights now claimed, is that civil and political rights require from a government only that (1) it shall not actively interfere with their exercise, and (2) it shall prevent others actively interfering with their exercise. It seems to me that many (at least) of these human rights are secured only if the government also (3) guarantees the social and economic rights which permit all men to exercise them. Otherwise, these civil and political rights will not be practicable, all men will not in fact be able to exercise them.

So much for Cranston's philosophical and political objections to the inclusion of social and economic rights in a list of human rights. Cranston would not deny that *some* welfare rights are human rights - the traditional rights to liberty and a fair trial are plausibly described as welfare rights. But he would deny that certain other, social and economic welfare rights are human rights. I have tried to meet his arguments to this conclusion because they seem to me to hinder the effective, i.e. statutory, protection of all these welfare rights. Where human dignity is used in moral justification of social welfare provision, we assume welfare entitlement to be a human right. It is this assumption which it has been my purpose to clarify and defend. It points us towards the Universal Declaration, and a framework for the welfare rights approach which matches its ambitions.

Part Three

Social welfare and social control

We began with the thought that modern social welfare
policies are to be understood as help given to the stranger.
I have gone on to discuss the kinds of justification which
might be offered for policies of giving to strangers. As we
have seen, justification may refer us to merit or, more
plausibly in the present case, to need. We have seen
that policies discriminating on grounds of merit provide
not only care but also *social control* - simply because the
undeserving are encouraged to acquire the meritorious
characteristics if what is withheld is something they
want. This may also be true of policies justified by
reference to need, when what the stranger needs is decided
by someone else. This latter point may come as a surprise.
Surely what someone needs can be 'objectively' determined,
so that when someone else decides what the stranger needs,
provided the person assessing need is a skilled professional,
the stranger cannot rationally disagree: there is no room
for loss of individual liberty or social control; any
rational man wants what he 'objectively' needs.

Unfortunately this is not so. Needs are identified by
reference to norms; what a man needs depends upon what he
ought to be doing; and what a man ought to be doing is not

a matter in which there are 'experts'. Let me enlarge.

The needs which seem least dependent upon norms are
such physiological needs as the need for food and water.
But even here the food and water are needed only if we
wish to stay alive. A man determined on suicide no longer
needs food and water. Other needs are more obviously
norm-dependent, for example a need for love and affection.
As Benn and Peters point out (1959, p.144), men can live
without love, but there is reason to believe that if they
have not had a certain amount of love in infancy they will
be unable to form lasting attachments, distractable,
incapable of being absorbed in anything for long, and so
on. These consequences of deprivation of love are evidence
of a need for love only if living in this manner is judged
to be undesirable.

Of course, most of us do judge staying alive to be
desirable, and living in the manner just described to be
undesirable. General acceptance of the norms upon which
the identification of needs is dependent disguises their
normative character and falsely suggests 'objectivity'.

Since what the stranger needs logically depends upon
what is regarded as desirable, when what he needs is decided
by someone else the point of satisfying the judged need
is to achieve a state which the decision-maker regards as
desirable. That is, he is directed towards goals which may
not be his own; in so far as they are not, he is controlled;
in so far as his goals are not sought or known, he may be
the subject of paternalism (see Weale, 1978). For example,
the need of a mental hospital patient for a strong dose
of a sedative might arise when hospital staff and other
patients regard it as desirable that he should be reduced to
a state of apathetic calm. If the patient does not see such

a state as desirable, to administer the drug is to control
him. Social welfare provision directed towards the needs of
strangers, or anyone else, may nevertheless be an instrument
of social control.

I want to turn in Part three from discussions of who to
help to discussions of when to stop; though we shall find
that such discussions are often related: characteristics
which make certain individuals worthy of care are often
what is thought to be defended by ending intervention.
However, we shall come to this. I want to begin by asking
'What ought to be the general limits of society's right to
intervene unsolicited in the lives of its members, through
social welfare agencies?' I discuss *unsolicited*
intervention, of course, because this is precisely the kind
of case in which the view that the individual needs something,
which intervention is intended to supply, is the view of
someone other than that individual and has been reached
independently of his view as to what is desirable. I shall
raise my question with particular reference to those social
welfare agencies involved in social work. This general
discussion, which introduces the liberal principles which
often play a crucial part in arguments against intervention,
will be followed by a discussion of moral issues arising
in the context of a particular form of intervention used in
social work and elsewhere: behaviour modification. In each
of these discussions, the arguments to limit intervention
make reference to valued human characteristics. In the final
discussion of Part three I will introduce discussion of
children's rights, to show that arguments justifying
intervention in their lives use closely related arguments,
though often drawing the wrong conclusions.

12   Freedom from welfare

Particular cases raise general issues. The cases of Maria
Colwell and Richard Clarke, (1) for example, raise general
questions about social work intervention management: *how*
should intervention be co-ordinated? Such cases also raise
general questions about the proper limits of social work
intervention: *when* should we intervene?

The second question is philosophical, but not therefore
only of importance to philosophers or teachers of social
work. It is also of importance to *practising* social workers:
particular cases (rationally dealt with) reflect general
practice, which manifests, to some extent at least, policy
decisions or general assumptions about when we ought to
intervene. Practising social workers answer this
philosophical question in practising social work. Of course,
general practices also manifest constraints which are not
the consequence of social workers' decisions or assumptions.
Resource restraints, for example, both financial and human,
are usually contested. However, my interest here is in
constraints of the former sort on social work intervention.
What constraints should there be? Has society the right to
intervene, through social work agencies, in the lives of its
members, and if so, on what grounds and subject to what

limitations? This philosophical question is also a *moral*
question, of course.

Since social work intervention may be welcome, unwelcome,
and lots of other things in between, and since also the
client's attitude to intervention may be relevant in
determining its proper limits, our grand question needs to
be a little less general if we are to cope. I shall discuss
only *unsolicited* intervention. Further, the discussion
will take the form of a defence of a position which has its
roots in J.S. Mill's essay 'On Liberty'. Mill asserts that

the sole end for which mankind are warranted, individually
or collectively, in interfering with the liberty of action
of any of their number, is self-protection...the only
purpose for which power can be rightfully exercised
over any member of a civilised community, against his will,
is to prevent harm to others. His own good, either
physical or moral, is not a sufficient warrant. He
cannot rightfully be compelled to do or forbear because
it will be better for him to do so, because it will make
him happier, because, in the opinions of others, to do so
would be wise, or even right (in Warnock, 1962, p.135).

Thus Mill marks the limits of justified intervention to
compel an individual to behave in one way rather than
another. Mill includes under the heading of 'compulsion'
not only physical force, but also 'the moral coercion of
public opinion': he does not include remonstration,
reasoning with, persuading or entreating as 'compelling'.
Whether or not these forms of intervention should be regarded
as forms of compulsion, with regard to *unsolicited*
intervention by social workers, I shall *initially* defend the
view that unsolicited intervention *of any kind* in the
affairs of an individual is justified if and only if there

is a danger of serious harm to others.

Any member of the oldest profession will tell you to beware of 'soliciting'. That is, it is a word whose use is such that though some cases are clear cases, others are not at all clear. Anyone who has had his face slapped will confirm this. Similarly, though many self-referrals may be clear cases of solicited intervention, and many admissions under mental health acts clearly unsolicited, in between is an area of intervention not so easy to classify. The same sort of feature afflicts the phrase 'a danger of serious harm'. Having noted these features of the view, however, I shall ignore them. It is not that I hope they will then go away, it is rather that I'm not sure they are weaknesses, and, in any case, I have plenty of other difficulties to consider.

Before I consider objections, we ought to know a little bit more. What are the practical implications? Consider the following three cases. Andrew McShiftie is brought before a Children's Panel, having stolen a bicycle. The social background suggests that this is the only offence Andrew has committed and that mother generally manages very well. We also discover that Andrew is eleven years old, has friends who have committed rather more offences, and that his father died three years ago, so that there is no man about the house. Suppose we judge that there is not a danger of serious harm to others but that a period of supervision by a social worker would be of help to Andrew, and perhaps also to his mother. Given this judgment, on the thesis I shall defend, unsolicited social work intervention is *not* justified. That is, compulsory measures of care, in the form of social work supervision would not be the recommendation.

Rumours reach you to the effect that Annie McHeftie has
been ill-treating her children. You call, and intervention
is clearly unsolicited. In this case, on the view in
question, unsolicited intervention *is* justified, since
there is a danger of serious harm to others.

Third case: Lunchtime O'Booze, bachelor, rumoured to be
ill-treating himself in the only way he knows how. You
knock, he is sober, and tells you to mind your Pink Elephant.
Again intervention is clearly unsolicited. If you judge
there is not a danger of serious harm to others, then on
the view I shall defend, unsolicited intervention is *not*
justified.

The practical implications of my position may be
uncontroversial in these cases. I am not sure. But in
any case its practical implications for more controversial
cases will emerge in the course of the defence.

The first point which may be made is that the
philosophical debate in which we are invited to take part
reflects innocence of the social structure within which
unsolicited social work intervention takes place: in
providing the statutory services connected with probation,
child care, national health and public health, the social
worker's unsolicited intervention is, whether she enjoys
it or not, part of the task which is laid upon her by society.

Certainly society does thus set the *legal* limits of
unsolicited social work intervention. But our philosophical
and moral problem cannot be avoided simply by recognising
this fact. The question to which I have supplied one answer
is not 'What unsolicited intervention *is* permitted or
required by law?' but 'What unsolicited intervention *ought*
to be permitted or required by law?' When we ask the second
question we are, among other things, asking for the scope

of existing law to be justified, and to describe its scope
is not to justify it.

However, reference to the law may not be entirely
irrelevant. The view which I am defending reflects my setting
great store by individual liberty. It might be suggested
then, that the autonomy of the citizen may be preserved
without the severe limitation of unsolicited intervention
which I propose, provided it is governed by law: Even if
there is no danger of serious harm to others, we might be
justified in intervening unsolicited if the client is in
danger of seriously harming himself - and all this without
threatening autonomy, provided unsolicited intervention
is governed by law.

Once stated in full, this point is clearly unconvincing.
The position of individual liberty is not so simply assured,
rather it is contingent upon the laws in question.
Unsolicited social work intervention might be governed by
laws which severely restrict the autonomy of the citizen.
There is nothing in the nature of law which secures that
autonomy.

Even so, the citizen may have more hope of autonomy
where unsolicited social work intervention is governed by
the law. This is because intervention may be open to
independent assessment and is set within a framework which
reduces the opportunity for the arbitrary use of state
power. Unsolicited intervention is then not dependent merely
upon the discretionary judgment of a social worker.

It is often asserted that unsolicited intervention should
not wait upon a proven breach of the law in cases concerning
the interests of children. So in these cases even what
is, after all, only the possibility of legal safeguards for
individual liberty, since it depends upon the laws in

question, would be removed. It may be said in support that
children suffering from all the minor degrees of neglect
would be virtually unprotected. And, what is more,
prosecutions and legal decisions are based on concepts of
crime and punishment, whereas much parental neglect is the
result, in one form or another, of incapacity.

The first point clearly cuts no ice. Anyone who values
individual liberty will not sacrifice it to the elimination
of what are admitted to be minor degrees of neglect. The
second point suggests that to make unsolicited intervention
wait upon a proven breach of law sets such intervention
within a context in which the individuals concerned are
held responsible. But in these cases, in one way or
another, the parents are not.

Again, the argument is unconvincing. It assumes that
legal judgments cannot take account of such mitigating
circumstances. This is plainly false. Further, even given
that the objector is right about the facts in most cases of
parental neglect, one might still protect the interests of
children from minor degrees of neglect by means which fall
short of unsolicited intervention not dependent upon a
proven breach of law. Parents in general might be offered
the help which would relieve the relevant incapacities.
Provided this service was widely publicised and staffed to
meet the demand, parents might then be held responsible for
the interests of their children. Protection of the interests
of children is again set within a context in which
individuals are held responsible, though mitigating
circumstances may be taken into account, and unsolicited
intervention in particular cases may be made to require
first a proven breach of law. However, on the view I am
defending, the law should not concern itself with minor

degrees of neglect.

It may also be argued that unsolicited intervention should not wait upon a proven breach of the law in cases concerning the interests of childlike adults. Particularly in these cases, it may be said, unsolicited intervention helps us to avoid the inhumanity of withholding help which is needed but not asked for. In support it may be suggested that there is an analogy with the problems of adolescents and their parents. We know that many adults actually manage their lives no better than teenagers, or even than much younger children. If parents are justified in unsolicited intervention in the interests of their children, and surely parents *are* justified in preventing their children from seriously harming themselves, then is not society also justified in preventing childlike adults from seriously harming themselves, if necessary by unsolicited intervention?

Again we should be unconvinced. If the adults in question are truly childlike, then this can surely be proven, and unsolicited intervention in these cases be brought within a framework of law. Further, and more important since the law is not necessarily the guarantor of individual liberty, this is no argument at all unless the analogy in question can be independently established. That is, unless it can be shown that these adults are childlike independently of the fact that they have a different view of their needs from ours, then we have not justified paternalism in these cases, we have simply imposed our view upon them.

Since law does not necessarily guarantee individual liberty, I should stress that I am not simply arguing that unsolicited social work intervention should be within a

framework of law. My aim is to mark the limits of justified
unsolicited intervention and the limits I have suggested
apply equally to closely law-governed intervention and
intervention at social workers' discretion: it guides
law-making and the exercise of discretion. The scope of
this kind of position may also be indicated in relation to
the claim that successful casework cannot include
unsolicited intervention. This is a claim about social work
practice: my position is one which would govern practice.
Even if successful casework could or does include
unsolicited intervention where there is not a danger of
serious harm to others, on my view it is not justified. I
might agree that the aims of the casework were valuable,
but the view defended marks *justified* means to those ends.
I shall consider just two more criticisms.

It may be argued that my position overlooks the facts
of social connectedness, that most patients have relatives
and dependents who will suffer grief if they die; that
many are breadwinners whose dependants will suffer poverty
and deprivation if they become incapacitated, or mothers
whose children may well suffer neglect if their health
breaks down.

The consequences here said to be overlooked are not
uniformly serious. The protection of individual liberty
might well be thought more important than sparing relatives
grief. This order of priorities is not absurd. It might
be thought that individual liberty might be sacrificed
where dependants will suffer poverty and severe deprivation,
but even in these and the other cases mentioned, it has not
been shown, nor is it true, that there is no alternative
means of maintaining dependants' welfare: a generous widows'
allowance might keep the lady well clear of poverty, if not
grief.

It might also be said that if we allow freedom from
unsolicited intervention except where there is a danger of
serious harm to others, we renounce the attempt to help
the patient who would be only too glad to accept medical
advice but for some fear which can be detected and relieved
by someone who knows what to look for.

Again, there seems no overwhelming reason why this must
be a consequence of adopting my view. Certainly defenders
of individual liberty will be chary of recognising a category
of unsolicited intervention which was *really* (when you know
what to look for) solicited: this might be seen as a slippery
slope. Even so, in cases like these, where one can establish
that intervention would be solicited were it not for some
unfounded fear or whatever, unsolicited intervention might
be acceptable. But that it is a case of this kind must be
established independently of the fact that help is not asked
for though we think it needed. Otherwise we have not shown
that it is *really* solicited intervention, we have, once
more, simply imposed our conception of personal welfare
upon them.

This latter point is important in cases like attempted
or threatened suicide. The position so far defended, barely
stated, precludes unsolicited intervention in attempted
suicides which are not seriously harming others. Since the
justified limits of unsolicited intervention embodied in
the view reflect a view of the extent to which individual
liberty should be preserved, it may be pointed out that some
threatened or attempted suicides do not manifest *choices* but
temporary instability or irrationality. (2) Unsolicited
social work intervention in these cases is not threat to
individual liberty.

This seems to me a good reason to modify my position and

I shall conclude by restating the initial view appropriately
modified: unsolicited intervention of any kind in the affairs
of an *autonomous* individual is justified only where there
is a danger of serious harm to others. I would also repeat
the point that that an individual lacks autonomy in a
particular case must be established, or, if matters are
urgent, must be a reasonable assumption, *independently* of
the fact that help is not asked for though we think it
needed. Otherwise we simply impose our view. Whether or
not one's assumptions are reasonable, of course, depends
very much on particular circumstances but, to supply examples,
I would say that, other things being equal, it is a
reasonable assumption that a young man, drugged and attempting
suicide, lacks autonomy, while an old man suffering severe
arthritis, taking the same course of action, does not. (3)

I said earlier that arguments to limit intervention on
moral grounds often make reference to valued human
characteristics referred to in other contexts to justify
welfare provision. This is borne out in the present
discussion. The liberal argument developed is an attempt
to argue that intervention should not occur when it
restricts autonomy (except as a matter of 'self-protection').
In the present discussion the nature of autonomy has not
been fully clarified, but it clearly involves the capacity
to make choices. Further clarification might take us in
various directions, but these might easily include

the ability to choose for oneself, and, more extensively,
to formulate purposes, plans and policies of one's own...
and to carry out decisions, plans or policies without
undue reliance on the help of others (Downie and Telfer,
1969, p.20).

Or again, clarification may include the assertion that

autonomy further includes 'the capacity to earn one's livelihood'. These further clarifications, of course, are taken from our earlier discussion of 'respect for persons' and 'the work ethic', respectively. Each presents what characteristic(s) an individual must possess to be worthy of care. If 'autonomy' is clarified in either of these ways, we use possession of these same characteristics both to justify provision and to limit it.

13

Ethics and behaviour modification

Given that needs are norm-dependent, we have seen that individual autonomy, clarified in various ways, is threatened by policies which allocate assessment of need to anyone other than the individual himself, whether or not that other person is a professional working in the field of social welfare. I want now to further illustrate and develop this general point by examining accounts of behaviour modification programmes, accounts which argue that there is no real threat. This will lead us into some comment on that philosophical chestnut, 'the free-will problem'.

In their theoretical writings, behaviour therapists tend to minimise the problematic nature of the question 'what behaviour ought to be modified?' It is a minor matter which shouldn't cause much difficulty. Behaviour therapists obviously don't claim that the question is of no importance in treating people. The design and administration of treatment requires that the therapist identify the behaviour to be modified before and during treatment. What such therapists tend to underestimate is the moral and political significance of the answers. The answers reflect a view of how an individual ought to behave in the relevant circumstances. Answers to such questions about human

behaviour are no more independent of moral norms than are
answers to questions about need. Behaviour therapy in
practice is set within moral and political philosophies
which could be made more explicit.

Let me illustrate the therapists' tendency to minimise
the moral and political significance of their practice, by
first asking 'what is a problem?' Behaviour therapy
presupposes problems. Behaviour to be modified is behaviour
which is a problem. How do we identify a problem? This
is what one influential therapist has to say:

> The concept of problem is employed by professionals
> and laymen alike to identify and label selected behaviours
> or conditions. The concept implies atypicality or
> deviance and is generally evoked when the behaviours or
> conditions to which it refers are somehow aversive to
> those who apply the label, and the implication is that
> the behaviour or conditions should ideally be modified
> or at least be different (Thomas, in Roberts and Nee,
> 1970, pp.202-3).

This passage is full of problems. 'The concept', says
Thomas, 'implies atypicality or deviance'. Does it? Greed,
shaving and acne are all problems, but none are atypical
or deviant. Again 'the implication is that the behaviour
or conditions should be modified or at least be different'.
Chess is full of problems but few chess-players would want
it any different. The account given, then, is not an account
of the concept of a problem, since there are many things
we call 'problems' which do not fall within the account.
Even if the account is true of the limited range of problems
dealt with by behaviour therapists, the account so far skirts
the moral and political details of who determines what the
therapist shall regard as problematic and attempt to modify.

Conscious of this, Thomas enlarges

No problem can be said to exist unless there is at least minimal consensus among those in the defining community. In voluntary contracts, such minimal consensus generally consists of the concurrence of client and professional that a given behaviour could be worked on as a problem. In nonvoluntary relationships, where the active consent of the client would not ordinarily be obtained for reasons such as legal constraints on voluntarism, some minimal agreement among the professionals who have legitimate authority is ordinarily all that is required (wherever possible, however, client consent should be obtained.) If the client is the only one who defines something as a problem, the focus of modification may be upon the alteration of his definition (p.203).

The earlier sentences of this passage suggest liberal answers to the moral and political questions about who identifies 'the problem'. The final sentence shows how professionalism can undercut liberal values. But even when the moral dimension of therapy begins to surface, it is typically not further explored, and the social and political dimension quite ignored. As Irwin Epstein has warned,

while behavioural theory rejects invidious labels for client behaviour, practitioners almost universally view their task as the identification and reduction of 'problematic', 'deviant' or 'maladaptive' *client* behaviour. In other words the client remains culpable. He is no longer sick. Now he is viewed as someone who 'does not adequately perform social roles'. Alternatively, he is someone who has not learned to 'manage' his own behaviour. And the legitimacy of institutionally defined roles and definitions of deviance remains unquestioned (in Jones, 1975, pp.140-1).

Thus the range of problems identified by behaviour
therapists as requiring their professional attention tends to
preserve the institutional *status quo*, concentrating on client
manipulation rather than manipulation of his environment,
making the client culpable rather than the institutions
within which he operates.

A more direct way of minimising the moral and political
significance of behaviour therapy, particularly in relation
to individual liberty and social control, is to deny the
possibility of individual liberty. Thus Martin Shaw declares,

the matter to be decided in the treatment situation is
not *whether* behaviour is to be controlled but where the
controlling forces lie and to what extent it is appropriate
for the worker to assume some part in these forces (in
Jehu, *et al.*, 1972, p.164).

It is here that the philosophical chestnut is uncovered:
as Shaw puts it, 'the age-old controversy concerning
determinism and freewill' (p.161). Many supporters of a
'behavioural approach', with Shaw, see it as 'wedded
inevitably to a determinist view' (p.161). Let me briefly
review the debate starting from Shaw's account, which begins
well: 'the determinist view, briefly stated, is that
behaviour, like all other events in nature, is lawfully
related to antecedent and attendant events and that such
relationships may be quantitatively described' (p.162). When
we say of someone that he did something *of his own free will*,
we imply that he could have acted otherwise: he could have
avoided doing what he did. But if human behaviour is
lawfully related to events we call 'causes', it is not clear
how any action that is done could ever be avoided.
Determinism and freewill seem incompatible. And thus
behaviour therapy cannot be a threat to individual liberty

simply because, wedded to determinism, it is committed to denying that we have the opportunity for choice in which talk of liberty or autonomy makes sense.

This conclusion makes discussion of the ethics of behaviour therapy, by therapists who would draw it, rather odd. They deny free will and yet suggest, as does Shaw, that we are in a position to decide whether it is appropriate or not for a worker to do this or that as part of therapy. If we lack free will, therapists are as unfree to decide between genuine alternatives as are their clients.

The idea that events may be lawfully related is certainly plausible, and tempting. It is a source of effective assistance. To quote a nice example from Epstein (in Jones, 1975): in one case, over a two-year period it proved impossible to cure neuro-dermatitis in a young woman patient because of her compulsive scratching of the area affected. The disability resulted in her getting lots of attention from her parents, friends and fiancé. They were instructed not to discuss her condition with her and to discontinue any physical attention - such as the fiancé's practice of rubbing in ointment! Within two months the compulsive scratching had almost ceased; within another month the skin complaint was cured. Reinforcement of scratching - the sympathy and attention shown - had been withdrawn, and the scratching stopped. This is just one example of numerous types of case in which behaviour modification programmes are effective and welcome.

On the other hand, practitioners in the field of social welfare have traditionally placed great value on client self-determination. As we saw earlier, for all his preference for professional problem-definitions, Thomas recommends obtaining a client's consent. But if determinism and free

will are incompatible, and behaviour therapy is inevitably
wedded to determinism, then consent cannot be freely given,
and self-determination is self-deception. As the hard-
headed Bandura declares, 'All behaviour is inevitably
controlled, and the operation of psychological laws cannot
be suspended by romantic conceptions of human behaviour, any
more than indignant rejection of the law of gravity can stop
people from falling' (1969, p.85).

This line of argument would lead us to deny the moral
and political significance of behaviour therapy, or any
other forms of intervention as a matter of social policy.
But the force of the argument turns crucially on the alleged
incompatibility of determinism and free will. I want now
to look at two arguments *for* compatibility. I shall
introduce one from A.J. Ayer (1954) very briefly, and at a
little more length, an argument from R.S. Peters (1958).

Ayer would accept the premise from which Shaw and others
begin: events are lawfully related, as cause and effect.
However, he does not conclude that we are unfree:

it is not, I think, causality that freedom is to be
contrasted with, but constraint....From the fact that my
action is causally determined, it does not necessarily
follow that I am constrained to do it: and this is
equivalent to saying that it does not necessarily follow
that I am not free (1954, p.278).

Ayer points out that in arguments of the type we have
reviewed, a move is made from saying that events are lawfully
related, to claims that events, including human behaviour,
are *governed by causal laws*. This mere *metaphor* suggests,
falsely, that causes constrain and compel. And, as Ayer
goes on, 'If I am constrained, I do not act freely. But
in what circumstances can I legitimately be said to be

constrained? An obvious instance is the case in which I
am compelled by another person to do what he wants' (1954,
p.289).

Thus to be wedded to determinism, to belief in lawful
relations between events, is not to be required to deny free
will. Behaviour therapists who take this *additional* step,
without other reasons for so doing, are simply misled by
metaphor. On the other hand, we can be constrained: not
by causes but by our fellow-men. We are constrained when
we are compelled by another person to do what he wants. And
it is this thought, I suggest, which tempts even those who
regard determinism as incompatible with free will,
inconsistently to continue to recommend a patient's consent.
A behaviour therapist who compels his patient to do what
he or some third person wants, constrains him: his patients
liberty *is* restricted.

R.S. Peters offers the following account of human
behaviour. If we are confronted with a case of a genuine
action (i.e. an act of doing something as opposed to suffering
something), causal explanations are, by that very fact,
inappropriate as sufficient explanations. *To ascribe a point*
to an action is, by that very fact, to deny that it can be
sufficiently explained in terms of causes, though, of course,
there will be many causes in the sense of *necessary*
conditions. But causal explanations may *rule out* what we
may call rule-following purposive explanations. To ask what
made Jones do something is at least to suggest that he had
no good reason for doing it. (1958, p.12). So causal
explanations are sometimes inappropriate, though not always

> instead of the omnibus question 'why did Jones do that?'
> we often ask what made, drove, or possessed him to do it.
> These are usually cases of lapses from action or failure

to act - when there is some kind of *deviation* from the purposive rule-following mode (pp.9-10).

Let me try to clarify some of the terms of this account. A purposive explanation explains by referring to purposes. For example, 'he went into the Chemist's to buy a bottle of Lucozade', explains what he did by referring to his purpose. Peters calls such explanations *rule-following* purposive explanations because there are limits to what can be *understood* as an attempt to achieve any particular purpose. For example, pouring cold (or hot) custard down someone's trousers is a way of showing him your anger and dislike and, however odd, would, other things being equal, be understood as such. Meanwhile, back in the Chemist's, if Jones dived head first through the shop window his behaviour would not be understood as an attempt to buy Lucozade, or anything else, and the assistant would not say 'Can I help you?' The man has broken one of the rules which characterise the activity of shopping, and the assistant would therefore not understand him to *be* shopping. In this way purposive behaviour is rule-following.

Rule-following purposive explanations are the first kind of explanation we turn to to tell us *why* Jones did whatever he did. And when they *are* explanatory - as in the case in which the question 'Why did Jones go into the Chemist's?' is answered by saying 'To buy a bottle of Lucozade', *causal* explanations would be insufficient. There might be causal explanations you could offer, but they wouldn't capture the fact that wanting to buy something is a *reason* for going into a shop, and that Jones acted for this reason, whatever else, in his past potty-training or his present environment, moved him. So, where rule-following explanation is explanatory, causal explanation is incomplete.

But rule-following purposive explanation isn't *always*
available to be explanatory. If a man really does dive head
first into a shop, we would not accept 'he's shopping' as
a rule-following explanation available in these circumstances.
The behaviour is outside the limits of what can be understood
as an attempt or part of an attempt to purchase goods. And
where we can find no alternative rule-following explanation
available which would explain and might be his reason for
behaving in this way (e.g. he's a plate-glass tester only
doing his job), we turn to causal explanation. As Peters
says, 'to ask what made Jones do that is at least to suggest
that he had no good reason for doing it...there is some kind
of *deviation* from the rule-following purposive model'.

All this allows determinism and free will to be compatible
because it allows that even if we were able to give causal
explanations for all human behaviour, for some human
behaviour such explanations are insufficient, and this
arises in cases where our behaviour not only has causal
antecedents, but is purposive, and not only caused, but
also for a reason. In such cases, had our purpose been
different, we could have behaved differently, and are thus
free, even though our behaviour has a causal history
whichever course it takes.

Further, Peters recognises that we do not always act for
reasons, not all behaviour is purposive. In these cases
causal explanation *is* sufficient. Determinism and free will
are compatible because though every event has a cause,
some events, some of our behaviour, but not all, occurs as
(part of) an attempt to achieve a purpose.

This account of human behaviour, if it is correct, shows
why the learning theories of behaviour therapists are useful
in practice and have moral and political significance in

relation to individual liberty and social control. In many
cases, the patient has reason to behave differently, but
cannot. He is not self-determining in this respect. Our
compulsive scratcher, discussed earlier, was like this. In
such cases, if change can be achieved by behaviour therapy,
provided the patient seeks such change, presumably because
the present behaviour hinders his present purposes,
individual liberty is not undermined, but is, rather,
enhanced. But even in these cases a moral question has to
be considered. Treatment of compulsions for which the
patient does not seek treatment may be an infringement of
his liberty - though it may be justified if others are
seriously harmed. Usually others are simply offended, and
this is less obviously sufficient warrant for intervention.

In many other cases an individual can be shown that a
change in his behaviour will serve his purposes: that he
has a reason to behave in the way desired by others. Though
he may have stronger reason not to do so, being quite
happy with his 'anti-social' behaviour because it serves
his 'anti-social' purposes, by reference to which it is
explained within the rule-following purposive model. In
such cases where behaviour modification could produce
socially acceptable behaviour, there is a danger of
replacing reasoning by behaviour modification, reducing
self-determination to the right to do what is wise, good,
'adaptive', and so forth, in the eyes of society. Of course,
reasoning may fail and constraints may be necessary. But
where social control is explicit, it is open to question.
If we turn to behaviour therapy to achieve socially
acceptable behaviour in such cases, control is disguised as
care, individual liberty sacrificed to social goals.

Learning theory is not theoretically hostile to client

self-determination, despite being wedded to determinism. But there is a danger in practice of the behaviour modification techniques it implies being used to extinguish client's behaviour based on socially unacceptable purposes. If this part of social welfare provision is to be seriously described as 'help' and not to be regarded as a tool in social engineering, behaviour modification must be restricted to behaviour *deviating* from the purposive rule-following model, and even here suit the patient's purposes.

As we saw in Chapter 12, Part three, discussions of social
welfare and social control tend to focus on moral and
political issues grouped around the notion of individual
liberty. My discussion of unsolicited social work
intervention and my discussion of behaviour modification
programmes had this focus. Developing the liberal
viewpoint, intervention was resisted where it would restrict
the client's opportunities to pursue his own purposes. This
kind of defence of individual liberty, I suggested, was
founded upon the moral view that our capacity for self-
determination is of great value, a key component in the
explanation of social policies caring for strangers.

In Chapter 8, Part two we saw that adopting principles
which I called forms of 'respect for human beings' entails
our valuing a wider range of human characteristics than just
the capacity for self-determination, and gives a broader,
and, in the case of *our* social policies, a more plausible
explanation of policies offering care to strangers.
Discussion of social welfare and social control might have
this broader background. Social policies usually restrict
or enhance a wider range of characteristics than just the
capacity for self-determination, and thus raise moral issues

grouped around all these valued characteristics. Social
control is not only opposed to individual liberty.
Paternalism is not only the promotion or restriction of
self-determination.

I turn not to the idea of childhood. Children experience
the most widely accepted form of paternalism, aimed to
promote a wide range of human characteristics. The part of
the idea of childhood with which I shall be particularly
concerned is the notion that there are certain individuals,
namely children, lacking certain valued human characteristics,
and capable of acquiring those characteristics as a result
of paternalistic intervention. Adults are held to be
justified in imposing control and their view of what the
child needs, principally on the grounds that the child
lacks self-determination, and so cannot be left to decide
his needs for himself. Precisely because this form of
unsolicited intervention to promote welfare *is* so widely
accepted *without question,* I shall develop a line of
argument which should at least make us re-examine the
relevant social policies in the fields of education, child
care, juvenile justice and so on. My discussion draws
heavily on the views of John Holt (1975).

Arguments in defence of self-determination often use
the language of rights, and we have seen in Chapter 9,
Part two that the idea that there are certain rights
possessed simply by virtue of being human, may be useful in
the moral appraisal of social policy. In the discussion
which follows, I begin with the question 'Do children have
rights?' and I will criticise a number of arguments used to
justify paternalistic social policies which deny them rights
which those upholding the policies in question do recognise
as human rights. Children have rights of at least two

distinct sorts, and I want to begin by distinguishing the
two. These are, on the one hand, *legal* rights, and, on the
other, *moral* rights. A legal right is an entitlement
created by positive law, the actual law of actual states.
For example, a parent of a child referred to a children's
hearing has a legal right to attend that hearing, created
by section 41(1) of the 1968 Social Work (Scotland) Act.
This Act is law, and were it not for the existence of that
Act, there would be no such *legal* right.

A *moral* right, on the other hand, is *not* an entitlement
created by positive law. I would argue, for example, that
the right to life exists and belongs to all men whether
or not any particular positive law recognises that right.
Moral rights and legal rights often overlap. To keep to the
examples used so far: surely a parent of a child referred
to a children's hearing has a moral as well as a legal right
to attend; and the moral right to life is recognised by
law in this country in laws prohibiting murder.

This overlap can lead us to forget the distinction, but
let me give an example where there is currently no overlap.
This brings out an important feature of the relation between
the two sorts of rights.

There is no legal right in Scotland, in any circumstances,
to practice homosexuality. It might be argued that in some
circumstances at least, between consenting adults in private,
there is a moral right. There is a legal right in the UK
in certain circumstances, to divorce. Some people argue that
this is immoral; in other words, that there is no moral
right.

In these cases, from someone's moral point of view, legal
and moral rights do not overlap. They bring out more clearly
that legal and moral rights are distinct, *and* that morality

can be a source of *criticism* of the law. It can be the
driving force behind calls for *changes* in the law. On the
other hand morality can be a source of *support* for the law.
In the earlier examples of the right to life and the right
of a parent to attend his child's Hearing, supporters of the
relevant laws would argue that this is how things are
and ought to be.

Moral and legal rights, then, are different. I'm going
to talk about children's *moral* rights. However, because
of the relation between moral and legal rights which I have
described, it should be clear that if we can show that
children have *any* moral rights, we will be in a position
to argue in support of laws which recognise them, or to
criticise laws which deny them.

I begin with an argument to the effect that children
have all the moral rights now known as *human rights*. It
may be that our list of human rights is based on our views
about human *needs* - the connection being that given a
certain view of human nature, or our natural capacities,
and a view about what a 'balanced' individual or a
'civilised' society would be like, we are in a position to
say what opportunities, what freedoms, human beings need in
order to develop these capacities. We list these freedoms
as human rights. Someone with a different view of human
nature or a different notion of a civilised society would
have a different view of human needs. But I don't want
to carry my discussion into these muddy waters. I shall
start from a list of human rights and argue that if children
do have all the moral rights presently known as human rights,
then they have far more moral rights than we usually admit.
I shall go on to look at arguments for giving children
short-ration. The arguments are familiar, but I think they

are still worth assembling, first to remind us that they
are part of a tapestry of argument and justification, and
second because some of them may be seen, on closer
examination, to be threadbare.

'Human rights' is a twentieth-century name for what has
been traditionally known as *natural rights* or *the rights of
man*. Since ancient times men have fought for these rights,
with words and the sword. The constitutions of practically
every state in the world today give at least formal
recognition to 'the rights of man'; they are the backbone
of our idea of a civilised society. Human rights are a
category of moral right. They are moral rights, as the
1948 United Nations Universal Declaration says in Article 2,
to which 'everyone is entitled...without distinction of any
kind'. So, whatever your 'race, colour, sex, language,
religion, political or other opinions, national or social
origin, property, birth or other status', you have these
moral rights. For the purposes of this argument I shall
concentrate on the human rights set out in the UN
Declaration. (1)

As I have said, the moral rights listed in the Declaration
are part of our idea of a civilised society, and men have
died in their defence. And these rights are still important.
The moral rights listed in the Declaration are not yet
legal rights everywhere. The United Nations cannot compel
their translation into law, but the Declaration is an
important moral stand in support of laws recognising these
moral rights, and against laws denying them. So, the
Declaration lists moral rights we claim, and want to go on
claiming. Here are five abridged examples -

1 The right to life (Article 3)

2 The right not to be subjected to arbitrary arrest or

detention (Article 9)

3 The right to a public hearing by an independent and impartial tribunal, in the determination of your rights and obligations and of any criminal charge against you (Article 10)

4 The right to take part in the government of your country, directly or through freely chosen representatives (Article 21(1)) (in discussion I shall call this 'the right to vote' for convenience)

5 The right to work (Article 23(1)).

I don't suppose any of *us* would want to give up these moral rights. Now, as I have said, human rights are moral rights to which everyone is entitled *without distinction of any kind*. So they are the moral rights of children as well as adults. If we look at the first two rights I've picked out, I don't think we would hesitate in assigning them to children as well as adults. We recognise that children have the right to life just like everyone else: we punish the murderers of children at least as severely as the murderers of adults. And we recognise that children too have the right not to be subjected to arbitrary arrest or detention: for example, in section 42(1) of the 1968 Social Work (Scotland) Act, it says 'it shall be the duty of the chairman (of a children's hearing) to explain to the child and his parent the grounds stated by the reporter for the referral of the case'. The referral of children cannot be arbitrary, there must be reasons, and the reasons made known. So, we recognise in law that children also possess the first two moral rights picked out. This is not true of the others.

Let us take them one at a time.

(a) Section 35(1) of the 1968 Social Work (Scotland) Act

explicitly denies children the right to a *public* hearing in
the determination of their rights and duties if the grounds
of referral are accepted. It says 'Any children's hearing
shall be conducted in *private*....' (emphasis mine). I do not
claim that this section was not framed with the best of
intentions. It is probably designed to limit the stigma
attached to referral to a hearing. My point is simply
that children are not admitted to possess a human right
commonly enjoyed by adults. It is true that the Press may
attend, but this must be regarded as not resulting in a
public hearing or their attendance would be in breach of
section 35(1).

(b) Section 1(1) of the 1969 Representation of the
People Act says that 'a person shall be of voting age if he
is of the age of 18 years and over.' Since the 'age of
majority' is 18, the law does not recognise that *children*
have the right to take part in the government of their
country through freely chosen representatives. Again,
children are not admitted to possess a human right.

(c) Finally, through a host of regulations governing
the employment of children, we refuse to recognise that they
possess the human right to work. In connection with this
last moral right I should perhaps stress, in order to avoid
misunderstanding, that to recognise the right to work is
not to impose a *duty* to work. Giving children this freedom
would not entail their being forced to go down the mines,
or deliver milk for Sloan's Dairies or whoever.

So here are three human rights which we refuse to admit
are possessed by children. There are many more, such as the
right not to be subjected to arbitrary interference with
one's privacy (Article 12), and the right to freedom of
movement and residence (Article 13).

If we are to deny millions of human beings these and other moral rights, we had better have very good reason for doing so. What arguments do we offer? Our most common argument is based on the idea that there is something silly about saying that someone ought to be allowed to do something which he would not be able to do even if you let him. Thus it would be silly to say that my dog ought to be allowed to play at Wimbledon. Dogs cannot play tennis. So there is nothing unfair about him not being allowed to play. In the same way, the denial of the moral rights in question can be unjust if and only if the children to whom they are denied could exercise them. But the exercise of rights demands certain skills. In general it requires the ability to choose for oneself, to fomulate purposes, plans and policies of one's own, the ability to carry out such plans with some degree of independence, in short, the exercise of rights requires the ability to be *self-determining*. (2) Children are not self-determining. Therefore the denial of these moral rights to children is not unjust. On the contrary, because they lack self-determination, the idea that we should recognise that children possess these moral rights is just silly. This is the first general objection.

What are we to think of this argument? Is it a good one? I don't think so, primarily because it is wrong on the facts. Its sweeping claim is that children are not self-determining. But surely we can all think of children who are skilful in one area or another, who very often choose for themselves and plan to do things, and do them, without undue reliance on other people - from buying ice-cream to house-breaking. Such children are not exceptional! These children *do* have the ability to be self-determining and therefore *could* exercise the moral rights in question if we recognised that they possessed them. The idea of recognising that children possess these rights is *not* silly, and our present denial may be unjust.

Of course, since children begin life at a very early age, it must be admitted that *some* children are not self-determining. And so we might be tempted to say that there can be no injustice in denying these moral rights to *very* young children. (3) But even in most of these cases there is a reason to recognise a related right.

As I have said, the United Nations Universal Declaration proclaims the rights in question as moral rights to which *everyone* is entitled, without distinction of any kind. Still, merely citing an authority is no argument, either for recognising the rights in question or ones related to them.

One argument for recognising related rights would be that the human beings in question - very young children, and older children and adults who are like very young children - *can* be self-determining *in time*. This may not be true of all these people, but it will be true of most. Babies can't do what you have to do in order to vote or in order to work, but in time they will be able to do these things - so even if it would be silly to give them the right to vote and the right to work, we could recognise that they possess certain *related* rights, namely the right to vote *when they are self-determining* (in the relevant respects) and the right to work *when they are self-determining* (in the relevant respects (4)).

In terms of *realistic* social and political change, we might move from our position of denying children the right to vote and the right to work, to a recognition of them as now possessing the related rights to do these things when they are self-determining. As I say, I think this would allow most children to enjoy these rights in full long before they do now. This would be a first realistic step towards what is, on the arguments I have advanced, the socially just situation, in which all children except very young children and others like them, possess the rights in question in full, and in which the children excepted now enjoy the related rights to vote and work etc. when they are self-determining.

Giving the related rights to all these children immediately, and to the exceptions who wouldn't possess the full rights in what I called the socially just situation, isn't an empty gesture. Giving someone the right *now* to do so-and-so *when he can* doesn't look as if you're really giving him *anything* now. But this isn't true. You are recognising that any treatment imposed on him which is likely to impair his development of self-determination is injust.

Giving older children the full rights and giving babies and others like them the related rights is also a way of recognising that a child's interests and those of his parent may conflict, and that it is not right that the parent's interests should always prevail, or that the parent should always decide *whose* interests should prevail. I shall mention in a moment Mia Kellmer-Pringle's suggestion of lay spokesmen for the child in such cases. Incidentally, despite raising the school-leaving age, we do of course recognise that *some* children have the right to work (16-18 year-olds and others at certain times of day), though for most children this isn't so. I think this shows, amongst other things, that we recognise the crudity of age as a criterion of capacity.

I've said that very young children and others like them
should be recognised to possess the *related* rights. We
might go further and give *all* children the *full* rights *in law*.
I suggest this first because any test we devise for
identifying children lacking the relevant capacities, or
any age limit we impose is, as now, in practice bound to
give incorrect results in some cases. Some children who
are self-determining will be judged not to be so. Children
who could exercise these moral rights will be denied them.
And if it is right that every human being capable of
exercising these rights should enjoy them, an injustice will
be done. Second, giving all children these rights in law
not only does justice to those who should enjoy them, it
does no harm to those who cannot. Very young children
who cannot exercise these rights cannot possibly be harmed
by them. (5) So much for the first general objection.

For those of us who admit that most children are self-
determining, but want to deny them the moral rights in
question, there is, fortunately, another common argument
available. It goes like this: Though children are, from an
early age, and increasingly, self-determining, they lack
experience. They will as a result make many mistakes, many
unwise choices and plans. Children can be protected from
the consequences of their unwise choices by denying them
certain choices, certain moral rights. In their own
interests then, children must be denied certain moral rights.

As John Holt urges (1975, p.66), the trouble with this
argument is that it applies equally to many adults. Most
adults in the course of their lives will make plenty of
mistakes. And I think, as regards adults, most of us would
agree that given any real choices and alternatives almost
everyone will manage his life better than anyone else,

however expert, could manage it for him, and that if and
when he does make mistakes, he will be quicker than anyone
else to recognise and change them. The only way we can
fully protect someone against *his own* mistakes and the
uncertainties of the world is to make him a slave. He is
then defenceless before *our* whims and weaknesses. Most
adults would prefer to take their chances with the world.
I think most of us would agree that they have the right
to make that choice, and so we ascribe to them the moral
rights in question, and many others.

We say this about adults, but we are reluctant to say
it of children. Why? We do not accept what we might call
'the argument from unwise choices' as strong enough to justify
denying the moral rights in question to adults, so why
should it be strong enough to justify denying these rights
to children? Without a *supplementary* argument with which
to answer this question, these grounds are too weak.

The supplementary argument may take the following form:
It is true of adults as it is true of children, that they
lack experience in certain areas and so lack practical
wisdom. But these things are a matter of degree. Children
lack experience to a greater degree than adults, and are
as a result, likely to make *more harmful* mistakes. The
consequences of children's mistakes are more likely to be
serious. This is why we should accept 'the argument from
unwise choices' as applied to children's moral rights,
though not to adults' moral rights.

It seems to me that the point made in this supplementary
argument is reasonable, but its force is weakened by the
following considerations,

1 We can reduce the likelihood of serious mistakes by
children by giving them responsibility much earlier. This

additional experience will help them cope better as they
reach the stage at which serious harm can flow from their
choices. Children who have taken responsibility for finding
the way home after a family outing, or for the decoration
of a living room will be better equipped to assess the
dangers of choosing to take drugs, for example.

2 Some of the mistakes can be made less harmful. For
example, the right to freedom of movement (UN Article, 13(1))
granted to adults, if possessed by children, allows them to
leave home, having nowhere else to stay. This can be very
dangerous. But if hostels for such children were available,
and such children knew of them and knew that the wardens
would not treat them as captives to be returned to their
owners, children might use them, and be in much less danger.

3 Further, we can make some harmful choices less
attractive. Recognising that children possess the right to
work, for example, might lead children to make the
apparently harmful choice of leaving school. But if schools
were more attractive, better staffed, better equipped and
subjects better taught, few children would choose to
leave. (6)

4 Finally, we should bear in mind the harm done by
denying children the moral rights in question, and others.
The right to freedom of movement and residence (Article 13(1))
is a good example. Children lack this freedom. If they had
possessed it, and we had given them somewhere to go, how many
of the 15,000 Scottish children affected in *new* cases dealt
with by the RSSPCC in 1973, (7) cases involving ill-treatment,
assault and general neglect, would not have been so seriously
harmed? Many of these children, I suggest, would have wisely
chosen to leave.

Of course not all these children were capable of such a

choice. Many were babies. For these children a suggestion
recently put forward (8) by the Director of the National
Children's Bureau, Dr Mia Kellmer-Pringle, might serve. She
suggests that independent lay spokesmen be appointed to speak
for the child in cases where the child can give no view of
his own wishes and interests. This recognises that the
child's interests and the parents' interests may conflict
and that the child's interests are not simply to be of no
account. Babies might then move from the parental home if
the spokesman could perhaps convince a Children's Panel
that this was in the best interests of the child. And of
course this might work in reverse. Just as older children
might choose to return to the parental home, if they were
welcome, so a spokesman might argue for a child to be
allowed by a Children's Panel to return to the parent's
home. It is perhaps also worth stressing the importance
of the independence of such spokesmen. They should be
independent of the parents, but also independent of the
local authority. So they should not be social workers, for
example. This is because the child's interests may also
be different from those of the local authority, a social
worker, a headmaster of a List 'D' school, or whoever.

The point made by the supplementary argument, that
children are likely to make more harmful mistakes, retains
some force, but I don't think it retains enough, in view
of the points I have made, to justify denying these moral
rights to children. Most people, I think, do believe it
retains enough force and would use the point to justify the
denial of children's moral rights. However, the pill is
sweetened by recognising children as possessing other moral
rights *not* enjoyed by adults. The most obvious example is the
right to free education (though Article 26 says *everyone* has

the right to free education), but there are others. The
treatment orientation of Children's Panel disposals recognises
a right not to be punished which is not enjoyed by adults.

That is all I want to say about the general arguments used
to justify denying that children possess certain moral
rights. I have said that I find them unconvincing but that
they are acceptable to most people. Thus, conscious that
my case will need to be quite strong if it is to shake
conventional wisdom, I should now like to discuss the two
rights seen earlier to be denied: the right to vote and
the right to work. Many of these very conventional arguments
have recently been gathered together by John Holt, in
'Escape from Childhood'.

First the right to vote. My first positive argument
for recognising this right as extending to children is an
argument which applies to all self-determining people, and
refers to a principle which most of those who would presently
disagree with me would accept. It is that 'to be in any
way subject to the laws of a society without having any
right or way to say what those laws should be is the most
serious injustice. It invites misrule, corruption, and
tyranny' (Holt, 1975, p.118). No supporter of democracy
can deny this. And thus, for any supporter of democracy
who would also deny children the right to vote, it puts the
onus on him to justify their classification as second-class
citizens. His natural recourse is to some version of the
first general argument I considered earlier, that children
lack self-determination. I have already said why this
seems to me to be too weak.

The other positive reason for giving people control over
their government, and so some control over their lives, is
that it may and probably will make them more informed and

responsible. People do not always learn from experience,
but without it they do not learn at all. And experience
alone is not enough; they must have not just experience
but the opportunity to affect experience. If they think
their choices and decisions make a difference to them, they
will have every reason to try to choose and decide more
wisely. But if what they think makes no difference, why
bother to think? It is not just power, but *impotence*, that
corrupts people....It makes them indifferent, lazy, cynical,
and irresponsible. (See Holt, 1975, pp.118-19.)

This is true of children as it is of adults. Indeed
this point turns the general argument which I called the
'argument from unwise choices' on its head. That argument
says that children should be denied the right to vote, and
other rights *because they are irresponsible*. It seems to
me plausible to suggest, on the contrary, that in so far
as it is true, children are irresponsible because they are
denied the right to vote and many other moral rights. We
are all inclined to dismiss children's claims to the right
to vote by saying that they don't understand the issues,
that they wouldn't know a good policy from a bad one. The
fact is that this is true of most voters and many MPs (e.g.
how many of us can say much about inflation?). We do not
think this debars us from voting, and so we shouldn't use it
to debar children of that right.

Next, the right to work. I have already stressed that
there is a difference between having the right to work and
being obliged to work. I am *not* recommending that children
be compelled to climb up inside chimneys, or crawl along
narrow mineshafts. On the other hand, I am saying that they
should be allowed to work if they want to. In the context
of these examples, even this may be controversial. Do I want

children to be able to choose to work in these appalling
conditions? Not at all. We protect adults from such
intolerable working conditions and we should protect children
too. Not by denying the right to work but by the regulation
and inspection of working conditions.

It might be said of course that this is all very well
for middle-class children. They may be able to choose not
to work. But if children did have the right to work,
children in poor families would have no choice, their
parents and their poverty would oblige them to work.

Again, I do not think the answer lies in denying them
the right to work. Rather we should tackle poverty. At
the moment we are in the absurd position of doing nothing
much to relieve poverty and making it an *offence* for
younger members of the family to do something to relieve
their poverty!

The right to vote and the right to work are two
important examples of the fact that the rights of man,
human rights, have become the privileges of adults. I have
tried to explain why most people, or at least most *adults*,
think that this state of affairs is fine, and I've also
tried to explain why I am not yet convinced.

Notes

2 SOCIAL POLICY AND ECONOMIC POLICY

1 The same extravagant error is made if we talk of
social services enjoyed as the 'social wage', as
did the Labour Government in the United Kingdom
under Harold Wilson, in its attempts to make 'pay
restraint' palatable.

3 SOCIAL POLICY AND MORAL OBLIGATIONS

1 I came across this term in discussion with Professor
R.S. Downie, who discovered it in the writings of
the late Rev P. Wicksteed.

5 ECONOMIC POLICY AND ALIENATION

1 The present summary takes points from 'The Causes of
Alienation' by Ernest Mandel, reprinted in Mandel and
Novack (1970). Incidentally, comment from my Glasgow
colleague, Scott Meikle, has reminded me of the
dangers of a-historical abstractions in this and any
other context of analysis. My discussion of 'economic
relations' is not meant to identify a type of relation
manifested in all societies, though in different forms,
but rather one manifest in our society, and which
offers, or rather allows, a significantly restricted
social identity: a form of alienation.

8 POSITIVE DISCRIMINATION AND SOCIAL JUSTICE

1 Thus I interpret the call for selectivity as a call for social policies favouring those with least resources to satisfy at least basic needs. It may be worth noting that the call is in fact ambiguous. It may be a call for social policies favouring those with greater needs, basic or otherwise, paying no attention to the level of private resources available to the individual, provided only that he has less than enough. For example, under this banner we might concentrate medical help on those who are most ill, even if they are almost able to manage without our help, and give little assistance to those who are less ill, even though they are quite unable to manage without our help.

2 My account of comparative justice follows Feinberg (1973), ch.7.

3 Graham Moran suggested to me that compensation implies commitment to equality and not simply to justice. Justice demands an end to unjust discrimination, but no more. This may be right, but surely justice also demands compensation if, as is usually the case, those suffering unjust discrimination continue to suffer its effects even when unjust discrimination has ceased. Here compensation aims at equality as a matter of justice by removing the continued effects of the injustice.

9 DISCRIMINATION AND SOCIAL CONTROL

1 It might be worth saying at this point that because Feinberg's test is concerned with individuals who are *responsible* for possession of the status-enhancing or stigmatising characteristic, any account of just discrimination, any account of the allocation of status and stigma determined by moral principles, will not help us to decide how to regard those many individuals who may be said to *slide* into states of dependency - in the context, perhaps, of bad housing, part-time education, frequent residential supervision, long-term unemployment, and so on - where it is difficult to point to any deliberate choices having been made.

10   WELFARE RIGHTS AND HUMAN RIGHTS

1   The Universal Declaration and the European Convention are reprinted as Appendices A and B, respectively, in Cranston (1973).
2   Articles 8 and 9 mention the protection of health, Article 11 proclaims the right to form and join trade unions, presumably for the protection of economic interests, and Article 2 of the first Protocol to the Convention adds the right to education.
3   Cranston (1967), p.50. The arguments recur in Cranston (1973) and R.S. Downie (1971), p.49. Except where otherwise stated, references to Cranston's work are to his 1967 article.
4   See Michael J. Hill 'Selectivity and the poor' in Townsend and Bosanquet (1972) and P.R. Caim-Caudle (1969 (1969).

12   FREEDOM FROM WELFARE

1   See Chris Andrews, Child Care Miscellany, 'Social Work Today' vol.5, no.14, 17 October 1974.
2   This objection, and my reply and subsequent modification of my position all rest upon the assumption that a distinction between what an individual chooses to do and what he is made to do can be sustained. Resolution of what is known to students of philosophy as 'the free-will problem' is crucial for the position which I adopt and defend in this chapter. Discussion of this problem comes in chapter 13, Part three.
3   Many of the criticisms considered are taken directly from Irvine (1964), views endorsed in Foren and Bailey (1968), pp.54-5.

14   THE IDEA OF CHILDHOOD

1   See Cranston (1973), Appendix A.
2   This account of self-determination comes from Downie and Telfer (1969), p.20. The account is, of course, very general, and it is worth remembering that (a) not all of the capacities that make up self-determination may be necessary for the exercise of all the human rights listed in the UN Declaration; (b) these capacities may not all develop and mature at the same time; (c) we might favour other capacities as qualifying one for full or related rights, such as the capacity for suffering. See Watson (1976).

3 This also applies, of course, to older children, and
   adults, who are retarded to the extent of being like
   very young children in their capacities.
4 Perhaps I should stress that I do not say that very
   young children, etc., should possess *only* 'related'
   rights. Even if we say that rights must be 'earned'
   by the possession of capacities, children would possess
   the right to life *in full*, because they are capable
   of breathing, etc. The difficulty comes with people
   who need to be kept alive. They lack the capacities
   concerned. If these people have the right to life,
   we must admit that not all rights need to be 'earned'
   by the possession of the relevant capacities.
5 If we decided not to give children the full rights in
   law, an appeals procedure could let injustices come
   to light.
6 I'm not saying that some education should not be
   compulsory. A certain kind of education must be
   acquired if a person is to exercise any rights, make
   any choices. Still, there might be a distinction
   between this kind of education and what goes on in
   some schools.
7 R.S.S.P.C.C. Report for 1973, p.19; in 1972 there were
   16,000. These figures are critically discussed by
   C. Peckham and M. Jobling, in a letter to the
   'British Medical Journal', no. 5972, 21 June 1975.
8 M. Kellmer-Pringle, Who is on the Child's Side?,
   Observer Review, 19 January 1975, p.24. This
   suggestion is now incorporated in the Children Act
   1975, ch.72, part III, sections 64-6.

Guide to further reading

Each Part contains within its Chapters references to sources
of further discussion related to particular points in
question. However, it may be useful to have some guidance
on philosophical material which will help in the further
exploration of some themes only introduced here.
This book is itself intended to introduce students of
Social Administration to parts of moral, social and political
philosophy. Those who want to explore philosophy more
broadly might take their first steps by reading 'What
Philosophy Does' by R. Lindley, R. Fellows and G. Macdonald,
(London, Open Books, 1978) and 'Reason and Argument' by
P.T. Geach (Oxford, Blackwell, 1976).
The relationships between the idea of a society, morality,
and welfare objectives can be pursued by reading three
essays by Professor Peter Winch: Nature and Convention,
'Proceedings of the Aristotelian Society', 1959-60; 'Human
Nature' in 'The Proper Study', ed. G. Vesey, 1971; 'Moral
Integrity', an inaugural lecture published by Blackwell,
1968. All three are reprinted in his 'Ethics and Action',
London, Routledge & Kegan Paul, 1972.
On human dignity, see G. Vlastos, 'Justice and Equality'
in R.B. Brandt, ed., 'Social Justice', Englewood Cliffs,
Prentice Hall, 1962. A useful 'sampler' on discrimination
might be T. Nagel, Equal Treatment and Compensatory
Discrimination, 'Philosophy and Public Affairs', vol.2,
no.4, 1973, and P. Taylor, 'Reverse Discrimination and
Compensatory Justice', Analysis, vol.33, no.6, 1972-3.
On the theme of individual liberty, Isaiah Berlin's
'Four Essays on Liberty', Oxford University Press, 1969,
will open many doors. B.F. Skinner's book 'Beyond freedom
and dignity', Harmondsworth, Penguin, 1972, discusses some of
the social implications of behaviour modifications through

operant conditioning. 'Beyond the punitive society', ed.
Harvey Wheeler, London, Wildwood House, 1973 provides
for an aversive response. 'Children's Rights', ed. J. Hall,
London, Panther, 1972 argues for the liberation of children.
Good luck!

Bibliography

AYER, A.J. (1954), Freedom and Necessity, in 'Philosophical Essays', London, Macmillan.
BANDURA, A. (1969), 'Principles of Behavior Modification', New York, Holt, Rinehart & Winston.
British Association of Social Workers (1973), A Code of Ethics for Social Work, Discussion Paper no.2, Birmingham, British Association of Social Workers.
BENN, S.I. and PETERS, R.S. (1959), 'Social Principles and the Democratic State', London, Allen & Unwin.
BIESTEK, F.P. (1961), 'The Casework Relationship', London, Allen & Unwin.
BOULDING, K.E. (1967), The Boundaries of Social Policy, 'Social Work' (USA.), vol.12, no.1.
BRANDT, R.B. (1962), ed., 'Social Justice', Englewood Cliffs, Prentice-Hall.
BROOKE, R. (1972), Social Administration and Human Rights, in P. Townsend and N. Bosanquet, eds, 'Labour and Inequality', London, Fabian Society.
CAIRN-CAUDLE, P.R. (1969), Selectivity and the Social Services, 'Lloyds Bank Review', no.92.
Central Council for Education and Training in Social Work (1976), 'Values in Social Work', Discussion Paper 13, London, Central Council for Education and Training in Social Work.
CHECKLAND, S.G. and E.O. (1974), eds, 'The Poor Law Report of 1834', Harmondsworth, Penguin.
CORRIGAN, P. and LEONARD, P. (1978), 'Social Work Practice under Capitalism', London, Macmillan.
CRANSTON, M. (1967), Human Rights, Real and Supposed, in Raphael, ed., 1967, and reprinted in Timms and Watson, eds (1976).
CRANSTON, M. (1973), 'What are Human Rights?', London, Bodley Head.

DOWNIE, R.S. (1971), 'Roles and Values', London, Methuen.
DOWNIE, R.S. and TELFER, E. (1969), 'Respect for Persons',
London, Allen & Unwin.
FEINBERG, J. (1973), 'Social Philosophy', Englewood Cliffs,
Prentice-Hall.
FOOT, P. (1967), 'Moral Beliefs' in P. Foot, ed., 'Theories
of Ethics', Oxford University Press.
FOREN, R. and BAILEY, R. (1968), 'Authority in Social
Casework', Oxford, Pergamon.
GEORGE, V. and WILDING, P. (1976), 'Ideology and Social
Welfare', London, Routledge & Kegan Paul.
GLENNERSTER, H. and HATCH, S. (1974), eds, 'Positive
Discrimination and Inequality', London, Fabian Research
Series Pamphlet 314.
GOULDNER, A.W. (1960), The Norm of Reciprocity, 'American
Sociological Review', vol.25, no.2.
GRICE, G.R. (1967), 'The Grounds of Moral Judgment',
Cambridge University Press.
HOLT, J. (1975), 'Escape from Childhood', Harmondsworth,
Penguin.
IRVINE, E.E. (1964), The Right to Intervene, 'Social Work'
(UK), vol.21.
JEHU, D., et al. (1972), 'Behaviour Modification in Social
Work', London, John Wiley.
JONES, H. (1975), ed., 'Towards a New Social Work', London,
Routledge & Kegan Paul.
MANDEL, E. and NOVACK, G. (1970), 'The Marxist Theory of
Alienation', New York, Pathfinder Press.
MAUSS, M. (1970), 'The Gift', translated by I. Cunnison,
London, Routledge & Kegan Paul. First published in Britain
in 1954.
McKEON, R. (1949), Human Rights in the World Today, in
'Human Rights Comments and Interpretations', UNESCO.
MOFFETT, J. (1968), 'Concepts in Casework Treatment', London,
Routledge & Kegan Paul.
PETERS, R.S. (1958), 'The Concept of Motivation', London,
Routledge & Kegan Paul.
PHILLIPS, D.Z. and MOUNCE, H.O. (1969), 'Moral Practices',
London, Routledge & Kegan Paul.
PINKER, R. (1970), Stigma and Social Welfare, 'Social Work'
(UK), vol.27, no.4.
PINKER, R. (1974), Social Policy and Social Justice, 'Journal
of Social Policy', vol.3, no.1.
PIVEN, F.F. and CLOWARD, R. (1971), 'Regulating the Poor',
London, Tavistock.
PRUGER, R. (1973), Social Policy: Unilateral Transfer or
Reciprocal Exchange?, 'Journal of Social Policy', vol.2, no.4.

RAPHAEL, D.D. (1967), ed., 'Political Theory and the Rights
of Man', London, Macmillan.
ROBERTS, R.W. and NEE, R. (1970), eds, 'Theories of Social
Casework', University of Chicago Press.
SOMERHAUSON, L. (1949), Human Rights in the World Today, in
'Human Rights Comments and Interpretations', UNESCO.
TAWNEY, R.H. (1937), 'The Acquisitive Society', London,
Methuen.
TIMMS, N. and WATSON, D. (1976), eds, 'Talking about
Welfare', London, Routledge & Kegan Paul.
TITMUSS, R.M. (1968), 'Commitment to Welfare', London,
Allen & Unwin.
TITMUSS, R.M. (1970), 'The Gift Relationship', London,
Allen & Unwin.
TITMUSS, R.M. (1974), 'Social Policy', London, Allen & Unwin.
TOWNSEND, P. and BOSANQUET, N. (1972), eds, 'Labour and
Inequality', London, Fabian Society.
VASEY, W. (1970), Social Welfare as a Human Right, in 'Social
Work Values in an Age of Discontent', Council on Social Work
Education.
WALLACE, G. and WALKER, A.D.M. (1970), eds, 'The Definition
of Morality', London, Methuen.
WALTON, R.G. (1975), Welfare Rights and Social Work:
ambivalence in action, in Jones (1975).
WARNOCK, M. (1962), ed., 'Utilitarianism, John Stuart Mill',
London, Fontana.
WATSON, D. (1976), The Underlying Principles, in F. Martin
and K. Murray, eds, 'Children's Hearing', Edinburgh, Scottish
Academic Press.
WATSON, D. (1977), Welfare Rights and Human Rights, 'Journal
of Social Policy', vol.6, no.1.
WATSON, D. (1978), Social Services in a Nutshell, in N. Timms
and D. Watson, eds, 'Philosophy in Social Work', London,
Routledge & Kegan Paul.
WEALE, A. (1978), 'Equality and Social Policy', London,
Routledge & Kegan Paul.
WILENSKY, H.L. and LEBEAUX, C.N. (1965), 'Industrial Society
and Social Welfare', London, Macmillan.
WILLIAMS, B. (1973), 'Problems of the Self', Cambridge
University Press.

Index